Turtle Heart

UNLIKELY FRIENDS WITH A LIFE-CHANGING BOND

ENDORSEMENTS

Honest, gritty, and well written. The story of a soul reaching to touch the face of God.
—**Jerry Eicher**, bestselling author of *When Hearts Break*, The Land of Promise Series

You will be mesmerized by the story of a shy, winsome Mennonite girl and her extraordinary friendship with an older Ojibwe woman. What they have to teach each other in their complex, fascinating connection is beautiful, startling, and wise. One of my favorite kinds of reads is a memoir that engrosses me like a novel, and that is exactly the kind of book you hold in your hands. Artful, gentle, funny, and true, Lucinda Kinsinger is a writer to watch.
—**Lorilee Craker,** NYT bestselling author of fifteen books, including *Anne of Green Gables, My Daughter and Me: What My Favorite Book Taught Me About Grace* and *Money Secrets of the Amish.*

In the clarity of her vision, the unusual insight and presence, the depth of observation and awareness, everything in Lucinda's honest account of her friendship with Char speaks of awakening—awakening through the process of loving someone. It is like an unexpected gift, full of surprise and delight, and the revelation of a hope long ago initiated but somehow never quite fulfilled—until now. In describing her relationship with an old, unfulfilled Indian woman, Luci's quiet, powerful story has awakened and fulfilled an old piece of my own heart. *Turtle Heart* is a uniquely beautiful book and a rare treasure.

—Mick Silva, writing coach and editor at Zondervan Books

Delightful and engaging, *Turtle Heart* held my attention throughout. Lucinda is honest and perceptive and connects with the reader on many levels. She is unafraid to address topics that are both difficult and complex, especially in the context of Mennonite culture.

—Katrina Hoover Lee, author of *Blue Christmas*, *Shatterproof*, and *Captain Garrison*

In a realistic clash of culture and age, an unlikely friendship forms. Surprised by a moral quandary, the reader is captivated. Stark contrasts of gentleness and crudity, innocence and shame, laughter and tears, love and hate, patience and anger produce a multi-colored thread that weaves this tender memoir.

—Timna Hooley, author of *Compassion, Making a Difference*

Turtle Heart is the history of an unusual cross-cultural, multi-generational friendship. Its finely drawn characters change slowly, realistically, with frequent relapses. They move inexorably toward a conclusion, where one of them must die. But I didn't want her to. By now, I loved her too much. *Turtle Heart* is a brave book about a courageous friendship; I didn't want to put it down.

—Sheila Petre, author of *Thirty Little Fingers* and editor of *The King's Daughter*

This is a story of old and young, of broken barriers and fierce love, of friendship and pain. This a winsome story of two brave hearts that come together, both needy, both strong. In it you feel the cold and bleakness of a winter day in Wisconsin and the groaning need of all humanity. In the next moment you feel warmth and light and joy. This is a redemptive story of questions with answers found only in the grace of Jesus.

—Luci Martin, blogger at *Three Green Doors*

Clear-eyed and honest, *Turtle Heart* is a brave, loving story of an unlikely friendship. Char and Luci find their way into your heart, and at the end you don't want to say goodbye.

—Amy Engbretson, columnist in *Keepers at Home*

Turtle Heart

UNLIKELY FRIENDS WITH A

LIFE-CHANGING BOND

Lucinda J. Kinsinger

ELK LAKE PUBLISHING INC

PUBLISHING THE POSITIVE
Plymouth, Massachusetts

COPYRIGHT NOTICE

Cover and Interior Design: Abigail Fowler, Derinda Babcock
Interior illustrations: Abigail Fowler
Editor(s): Sue Fairchild, Deb Haggerty
Author Represented By: Credo Communications LLC

PUBLISHED BY: Elk Lake Publishing, Inc., 35 Dogwood Drive, Plymouth, MA 02360, 2021

Library Cataloging Data

Names: Kinsinger, Lucinda (Lucinda, Kinsinger)
Turtle Heart: Unlikely Friends with a Life-Changing Bond / Lucinda Kinsinger
316 p. 23cm × 15cm (9in × 6 in.)
Identifiers: ISBN-13: 978-1-64949-303-3 (paperback) | 978-1-64949-304-0 (trade paperback) | 978-1-64949-305-7 (e-book)
Key Words: Friendship; Disfunctional Family; Aging; Mennonite Memoir; Homosexuality; Salvation; Mennonite Culture

Library of Congress Control Number: 2021944458 Nonfiction

DEDICATION

For Kathy, who loved her too.

ACKNOWLEDGMENTS

First, I want to acknowledge my heavenly Father, who gave me this story and helped me to write it.

Thank you to Naomi Newman, who gave me courage to write the book, who read it before anyone else did, and who made me believe that I was a writer.

Thank you to my parents, who believed in me and in this book when I had given up belief, and to my husband Ivan, whose support and insistence that it was time to move forward brought this book finally to publication.

Thank you also to Mick Silva, who gave me early editing help and the faith to believe my words would go somewhere.

To my agent Karen Neumair, thank you for giving this newbie a chance.

To Deb Haggerty, Sue Fairchild, Derinda Babcock, and the team at Elk Lake Publishing—thank you for making the book a reality.

To all my beta readers and those who gave endorsements: I appreciate your time and input so much. And to all future readers: I see you. This book is yours.

AUTHOR'S NOTE

I am sharing with you Charlene's and my story as I remember it, and as I perceived and recorded it at the time in dozens of journal entries and a taped conversation. Almost as long as I knew her, I wanted to write a book about her, and those early efforts to record evolved into a project spanning years. Though I have tried to maintain as much accuracy as possible in a work of this sort—built as it is from memory and perception—I could not place every incident in exact chronological order and used some liberty in arranging incidents according to where they fit in the larger theme of things. I also changed some names to protect privacy.

Know this as you read: Heraclitus taught—and Plato repeated later—that a river is never the same the second time you step into it. Every day, every minute, a new river flows. This story is a part of my journey, but I do not maintain every opinion expressed here in exact and unshifting form. Yesterday, I learned. Today, I learn more. And time has a way of adding perspective to things. Read this story, not from the perspective of the all-knowing future, but from the perspective of being there in it, with me.

I heard the F word for the first time when I was twenty-four. I was sitting in a college class—a foreign world, a planet away from my home—and heard the word spoken by a brazen student, an army veteran who was a bit older, more hardened into his personhood, more assured than the other students.

My professor looked uncomfortable. "I think we need to be respectful of other people's beliefs and not say words that might offend them."

He did not look at me, but I knew he thought I would be the person offended.

I was aware of myself—my shy, sweet face, bland and frightened at my table in the back corner of the room, my long dress specially sewn with an extra layer over the bodice to ensure modesty, my white mesh Mennonite head covering. My clothes have always made me stand out.

But this word—a cute little word—sounded harmless enough. Why should I be offended? I went home and looked it up in my big *American Heritage Dictionary*, and then I understood.

That was the year I started asking questions. *Is there a God? How can he have created hell if he really loves people? Is homosexuality a sin?*

That was the year I met Charlene, and she asked questions too. Her eyes grew intent and her brows angry when she asked me this question one day: "When Adam and Eve sinned, why didn't God destroy them and start over?" I knew she was thinking of all the evil on the earth, generation upon generation of it piled high and stagnating, maggots and retch and filth pouring out, blistering everything it touched.

"Why?" she asked again and again when pain pinched her legs, grabbed her insides, and twisted—hard.

"Could God forgive a murderer?" she asked another day. This time her face remained still and quiet. Waiting.

I knew the answer to that question. "Of course he could forgive a murderer. He forgave Paul, and he murdered people." But maybe my answer seemed too simplistic, unsatisfactory, for she asked it again later.

Charlene was a different sort of friend than I had ever had before. The first friend I had who drank. The first who swore. The first who told me how it felt to smoke weed, how first you get the happies and then you get the munchies.

I liked to look at a certain picture of her when she was young, maybe twenty. She stood with her chin profiled against the sea, a hippie bandana tied around her forehead and her shirt loose, something brittle and defiant in her face. The photo told me something about who she used to be before she became a frail old lady who hurt when you touched her.

I thought it strange sometimes, the way I loved her. Growing up Mennonite—the kind who wear long dresses and coverings on their heads and believe in staying separate from the world—I had somehow believed Mennonites were not like other people. I thought we had different emotions, different thought processes, different driving forces from everyone else. Before I met Charlene, I would never have opened up to someone outside my circle because I assumed they could not understand me.

Although I won't say she understood me. Not exactly. But our misunderstanding came from our two different souls, complete and unique in themselves, not from our different backgrounds. Our understanding came in the same way, reaching across time and space, perfect and untouched by circumstance.

Outwardly, we were different on almost every level—one young and one old, one sheltered and one tough, one shy and one feisty. And yet, in the center lay a spot where we connected, where we shared nerve and muscle and bone like conjoined twins. At that place in our center, our hearts beat as one. Charlene understood me in a way the old ladies in church—with their quilts and their gardens and their smug satisfaction with life—could never understand.

She asked me another question once, a question that opened my eyes to something I had not known existed in the world.

"Will you be my helpmeet?" she asked.

But that comes later in the story.

PART ONE—THE BIRTH

I met an old lady
wrists fine as bone china
her eyes black
and her hair black
as crow's wing
but her heart was red.

Seventy years before I met her—when Jews wore stars in Europe and Ojibwe worried over treaty rights in Wisconsin—Charlene was born. Given to a drunk Dutch papa and a "half-breed" Ojibwe woman, she made her entrance into the world against doctor's orders. Her mother was sickly, and after six children, the old country doctor had advised a cessation.

"But my father," Charlene told me, "being a young Catholic man, and not having any other form of entertainment other than getting drunk on the weekends … well, that's how I got born."

She was the seventh of an eventual fourteen. Her parents had expected a boy, whom they would call Charles Ray. When a puny girl entered the world, they called her Charlene Rae instead. She was so tiny her first crib was an old cigar box.

Her mother, being ill, had a long stay in the hospital while Charlene's Dutch grandparents, Grandpa and Grandma Brand, offered temporary care. At the time, they also cared for her grandmother's grandfather, Charlene's great-great-grandpa Dederich. He was an old man, eighty-five or so, and senile. He fell in love with baby Charlene and decided she was his. When her parents came to pick her up, he wouldn't let her go.

Then, there was another matter to consider. Charlene had been born with infantile scurvy and had to be fed bananas to make her well. Charlene's parents couldn't afford to buy bananas as the fruit at that time was quite expensive—a penny apiece. They talked it over, and between Grandpa Dederich's desire and the necessity of bananas, it was decided that Charlene would stay with her Grandpa and Grandma Brand.

At least, this is what Charlene was told, and what she told me.

I asked her once how she felt as a girl to be palmed off to her grandparents.

"I thought I was the luckiest girl in the world," she said, "to have two sets of parents."

Charlene's grandparents on her father's side were Dutch and on her mother's side Ojibwe and French Canadian. This made Charlene only a quarter Ojibwe. As long as I knew her, however, she referred to herself as Indian, a tribute to her respect for her mother and pride in her heritage.

Ojibwe oral history tells us that many strings of lives ago the Anishinaabek, or "original people," migrated from the east in search of the food that grows on water. This migration occurred over generations of time. Many splits and seven stopping places later, the tribe had settled in a wide swath around the Great Lakes, where they followed the *mide* way of life: organizing themselves into clans of Loon and Fish and Bear, harvesting the wild rice that grew in abundance, and living in harmony with the land and seasons.

The advent of the white man changed their way of life.

In the early 1800s, Michael Cadotte, son of a French man and an Ojibwe woman, married an Indian princess and established a fur trading network on the south shore of Lake Superior. He was the first white man to hunt the land along the Flambeau River, land that later came to be called Rusk County. Some say the French and Canadian fur traders who followed Michael called the river Flambeau, or "flaming torch," because they observed the Ojibwe spearing fish by the light of torches tied to their birch bark canoes.

The white men, it seemed, were always naming things.

In 1836, they named Wisconsin a territory.

In 1842, they named the agreement that ceded the Flambeau River Valley and much other Ojibwe land to the US government the Treaty of La Pointe.

In 1847, they named the first white child born in the area of Rusk County Myrtle.

In 1848, they named Wisconsin a state.

In 1884, they named a small town located in the Flambeau River Valley Weyerhaeuser.

The town was platted by Frederick Weyerhaeuser, the German lumberman who had come to America as a penniless, seventeen-year-old immigrant thirty-one years before. Mr. Weyerhaeuser bought up huge tracts of virgin pine in the Chippewa and Flambeau River valleys—majestic, silent forests, carpeted in pine needles and with no obstructing underbrush. When he left the Flambeau Valley ten years later, he was the richest man in America—valued at a hundred million dollars—and all the virgin pine in Rusk County was gone.

Charlene's great-grandmother was born during this lumber boom, in the late 1800s.

"She was a person I wish I had known," Charlene told me once. "She spoke no English, only Ojibwe, and she didn't believe in airplanes."

"How could she not believe in airplanes?" I asked, amazed. "Couldn't she see them?"

"When one flew overhead, she wouldn't look up."

I was born forty-five years after Charlene in the same Rusk County town, in the same small-town hospital, but the world I came to was a different world. My parents were Mennonites, descendants of German and Swiss Anabaptists.

I was the third of eight children, and the most memorable thing I've been told about my birth is I was born late on the night before Halloween, and the doctor came in dressed as a clown. As they did for each of us, my parents chose my name carefully for its meaning. Lucinda, which means light bringer, and, for my middle name, Joy.

My great-grandpa on my mom's side came to Rusk County in 1931, the third of four Mennonite families to move from Pennsylvania and settle in the area. According to a history written by my grandpa, "Four brethren of an adventurous nature decided to go west."

They came to the vast cutover which followed the lumber boom. The land consisted of massive stumps—Grandpa can remember stumps the size of tabletops—boulders, brush, swamp, second-growth trees, and rocks by the wagonload. Land was cheap and good for farming but clearing the land proved to be backbreaking work, demanding huge amounts of dynamite and determination. Bedbugs and mosquitoes were unconquerable, roads primitive.

Those four Mennonite families who came to Rusk County made up one of the first Mennonite churches in Wisconsin. Eighty years later, during my time, Mennonites were scattered throughout the state.

MARCH 2011

I peer through fog and darkness, searching the beam of my headlights for the house number. *424, 413, 411 ... ah, there it is.* But I've already passed in the darkness. Give me a car, and I will get lost. I passed the same road three times once, forgetting in the short time it took me to turn around, that, yes, I needed to turn there, and sailed on past, my head in a cloud.

This early in the morning, the streets—clouded white from their frequent salting during Wisconsin's long winter—are empty. I back up and pull into the driveway of 411 Lindoo Avenue. The mint-green shutters on this white cracker-box house make it unique.

I check my clipboard again: Charlene Brand. She's headed to the Barron hospital. I already know, from a conversation with Grandpa, that she receives regular dialysis treatments, a process where her blood is pumped through mechanical filters in place of her kidneys, which no longer function.

Grandpa is the one who introduced me to this transport job. Recently returned from teaching school in another state, I've been looking around for a job I can pursue while writing. Grandpa volunteers for the government-funded Indianhead Transit, picking up old, sick, and disadvantaged people at their houses and taking them to doctor appointments or grocery stores. He receives payment for his mileage, but not for his time. *I don't mind about the time,* I thought, when he told me. *I'll take my writing along.*

And so here I am, waiting outside Charlene Brand's house in the darkness.

"She's a spicy one," Grandpa said in his gruff voice when I told him I would be driving her today. He chuckled—his chin up and chest thrust out in the posture my family calls the Martin posture. One might think a person who stands like that is snobby, only Grandpa isn't. Or bullheaded ... he might be that.

"One time," Grandpa continued, "I told Charlene, 'Well, it looks like we're going to get Indian summer.' And she said, real snappy, 'You white men think you can get whatever you want, but this year the Indians aren't going to give you an Indian summer!'" He chuckled again. "I like her, but she's a spicy one."

A friend who also drives for Indianhead seconded Grandpa's warning. "She was real nice the first couple of times I drove her, but all of a sudden, she turned mean."

Their warnings intrigue instead of worry me. Charlene sounds like a challenge, and I like challenges when it comes to people, like to feel the pleasant power of shy smiles and diplomacy in winning hearts. I know how to handle demanding old ladies. They need to feel they are in control and need a bit of petting. With those two requirements in place, these old ladies are as pleasant as popcorn.

Does she know I'm here? Should I go to the door?

When several minutes pass and no one comes out, I walk down the concrete path to her house, up two cement stairs, and knock on her door.

Charlene, when she opens the door, is not the old lady I expected. She is wrist-thin and as short as a twelve-year-old, engulfed in a tan coat and bulky fur cap. Instead of gray, curled coifs, her hair is black and short, with one wispy streamer that trails down her back like the tail of a limp garter snake. Her face is narrow and brown, her dark eyes slanted at the corners. Small rimless glasses give her a look of class and intelligence.

Holding the doorknob for balance, she steps carefully onto the cement porch. "Burr-ito! It's cold out here."

I introduce myself, smiling. Charlene smiles back, white teeth flashing, eyes snapping to life like a spinning pinwheel at the fair. Our spirits meet in the frosty air between us and shake hands.

I like her immediately ... only it's more than a liking. I am drawn to her in the same way I must have been drawn to color and sound when I first opened my eyes to the world.

I turn to lead the way down the steps.

"Aren't you going to take my bag?" Charlene demands.

Her tone of voice does not offend, but instead delights me. I take her bulging blue tote and hook it over my shoulder. Charlene holds the mint-green railing in both hands and descends the two cement stairs one slow, lurching step at a time. At the bottom, she looks at me.

"Give me your arm."

She isn't demanding, exactly, but authoritative—a wren of a general directing her army.

Up close, she smells of cigarette smoke—a smell I might consider undesirable on others, but on Charlene, find atmospheric, like reading a mystery novel.

With her hand in the crook of my elbow, we snail to the car one excruciating step at a time. The blue tote keeps sliding off my other shoulder until I clamp it under my arm. I open the passenger door, and Charlene slowly places one leg inside and drops into the seat. Then, using both hands, she lifts her right leg into the car. The simple task of getting into a vehicle has never looked so difficult.

"The Ojibwe have a saying about the fog," Charlene says as we back into the foggy street. "They say, 'The Creator sent the clouds to earth.'"

The saying delights me, as everything about this woman delights me. She is bossy and opinionated—I can tell this already by her brief, well-articulated commands—but I think she speaks with a sort of humor, as though she finds herself amusing, as though her own vehemence is a game she plays with people. I bend every bone in my body to meet and to please her, and her spirit responds to mine, her sparkling eyes reflecting my delight.

Conversation rises easily between us as I tell her about myself and my family and ask about hers. She speaks with a simple dignity that gives weight to her words.

When the conversation falls silent, I turn on the CD player to soft gospel music—a Mennonite group singing a cappella, their voices soft and harmonious. It is the sort of music I like, the tradition I've grown up with.

Charlene listens in silence, her back straight against the seat. "What is your idea of heaven?" she asks suddenly.

At first, I stumble over my answer. What does she mean exactly? From all the verses and sermons I've heard over the course of a lifetime, I pull out words, line them up, and try to make them meaningful.

"Heaven will be beautiful ... more beautiful than anything we can imagine. And there won't be any sin there. You know all the suffering and sadness on this earth ... there won't be any of that in heaven."

"Well," Charlene says, "my idea of heaven is being able to take care of all the little baby animals."

We talk about God then. Charlene calls him the Creator, and I like that term. It holds something of ancient Indian drums in its tenor.

She tells me a story, speaking slowly, the spaces between her words adding significance. I picture a circle of Natives around a fire, weighing out wisdom in stories. Charlene would fit there, in the darkness and firelight, weaving suspense with her words.

"When our little brother was dying of cancer, my sister Mary called and told me, 'I don't believe there is a God. If there is a God, why is he making Ollie suffer and die like this?'

"'I don't believe God is the one making Ollie suffer,' I told her. 'It's the devil.'

"'But God is letting the devil do it,' she said.

"'Well, Mary,' I said. 'Let's suppose you could bargain with God. Let's say he told you he would let Ollie live if someone else would die for him. Suppose he gave you that choice—you had to choose someone to die instead of Ollie. Who would you choose? Which of our brothers? Which of our friends?'"

Charlene pauses and looks at me, the dark eyes with the slanted corners intent, ready to deliver the punchline. The fog has lifted now, and the sky has lightened outside the window. I slow as I near the corner in the village of Cameron and flip my blinker to turn left.

"Of course, Mary couldn't make that choice. No one could make that choice. I told her, 'That's why we have a God, to make those choices for us.'"

Charlene learned her faith from her mother. Her father didn't have much use for religion, she tells me later in our relationship. He would take her mom and the children to Mass, drop them off at the door, and go find a parking place. That, Charlene tells me, was his excuse not to come in.

Besides attending Mass at the Catholic church, Charlene attended Catholic school, which she calls the Nunny-Bunny School. Discipline was strict. Girls wore dresses and swearing was not allowed.

In the early sixties, when Charlene was in her twenties, Pope John XXIII implemented Vatican II, bringing sweeping changes to Catholic practice. Charlene grew disillusioned with the Church, not understanding why so much of what had been taught as unchanging truth was suddenly invalidated.

At some point, she converted to Lutheranism, was rebaptized, taught Sunday school, and sang in the choir.

She grew angry with the Lutherans when she was reprimanded by the minister for taking part in a Catholic communion service.

"Does God change from the Lutheran church to the Catholic church?" she demanded.

When her sister came to visit and was not allowed to take part in the Lutheran communion, Charlene got up, walked out, and never went back.

By the time we meet, she has formulated her own brand of religion, a smorgasbord of Christian beliefs and Native teaching. She takes from both freely, unaware of any contradictions.

"Do you believe in Jesus?" I ask her.

Charlene considers. "Yes, the Ojibwe have taken the Creator's Son, Jesus."

But when I mention the Bible, she snaps, "The Bible is just a white man's book!"

"Have you ever read it?"

"No, and I don't need to. It's something the white men made up."

"The men who wrote the Bible were Jews," I tell her. "Brown-skinned people like the Arabs in the Middle East. They were all different sorts of men—fishermen, shepherds— just normal people like us. You should try reading it sometime. It's interesting. I think you would like it."

I drop the point, knowing instinctively not to push, and the conversation moves on. But on the way home from the hospital, I mention it again, making my voice light and easy.

"You should try reading the Bible sometime. I think you would like it because you're a thinker and a believer."

"Hm." Her eyebrows rise, intrigued.

MAY 2011

Several months later—after I wonder if I'll ever see her again—I am once more assigned to drive Charlene. The air feels spring-cool against my cheeks as I walk to her door.

This time, she wears a shiny blue windbreaker set with a square white logo—*Waukesha Cutting Tools*—and a camouflage cap pushed onto her scruffy black head.

"I'm Luci." My smile stretches wide, friendly. Does she still remember me? "I drove you once before." A button of anticipation flutters in my stomach.

Charlene nods but does not smile.

The magic is gone.

Out on the highway, she scolds me for driving too fast in the early morning fog and darkness. "You shouldn't be going over forty in this."

I slow the speedometer to fifty—anything below that is just too extreme—give up trying to make conversation and flip on my soft gospel music.

Charlene listens a few minutes in silence, seeming to absorb the music. "I have a question for you."

"Yeah?"

"In the eyes of the Creator, would it be wrong for me to quit dialysis?"

"Quit dialysis?"

"When I'm on the machines and my toes start curling, that's when they know it hurts too bad and they should take me off. The other week when the doctor came in, I asked him, 'Why can't you put me on a morphine drip and let me die?' 'I can't do that,' he said. 'Part of the oath we take as doctors is to preserve life, not destroy it.'"

"But morphine doesn't kill you, does it?" I ask.

"Yes, it does. It gets to be too much for your body, and"—she slashes at her throat with pointed fingers—"you're dead."

But the doctor, she says, also told her if she chooses to quit dialysis, he will give her morphine to ease the pain of her inevitable death. At that point, it will be an end-of-life measure.

"I asked my family if they'd be okay with me quitting. They said it could only be my decision, and they'd support me, whatever I did."

By family—since she never married or had children—Charlene means her thirteen siblings. She told me about them on our first dialysis trip, her voice warm. "The Creator's purpose for my life is to take care of my brothers and sisters," she said.

Now, I try to imagine telling one of my sisters it would be okay to quit treatment and die. "Sure, sister, if that's what you want, I'll support you." I could never say that! I wonder if Charlene's family cares about her as much as she seems to think they do.

"I don't know if it would be wrong for you to quit dialysis, but if the morphine actually kills you, wouldn't that be suicide?" I offer more words, a vague floundering of them to prove that, really, I don't know. But my gut instinct screams no and every word I give insinuates that such an act would be suicide. This woman can't die. I haven't gotten a chance to know her yet.

She tells me then about her miniature schnauzer, Nibaa Ikwe, a flop-eared, shaggy-haired creature.

"We share a hairstyle," she says, pointing at her own scruffy head.

I laugh. "What does her name mean?"

"It's Ojibwe for 'Sleeping Girl.' My sister gave her to me the Christmas before last, and all she wanted to do was sleep, all curled up in her box."

"Nibaa Ikwe—sleeping girl. Teach me some more Ojibwe words."

She considers my request across a long pause. "Well, 'sugar' is 'si-si-bakwat.'"

"Si … si … bakwat," I repeat, trying to get the pronunciation right. "Si-si-bakwat."

"The Ojibwe name all the parts of a thing. If they want to say 'gooseberry pie' they don't just say 'gooseberry pie.' They say, 'flour, sugar, water, gooseberries.'"

"Teach me another word."

She tips her head, thinking. "Well, tomorrow you can tell your mom, 'Yippee-ki-yi-yay.' That's 'Happy Mother's Day.'"

"Yippee-ki-yi-yay," I repeat, and laugh. "I like it. It sounds like a cowboy yell. Yippee-ki-yi-yay. Yippee-ki-yi-yay."

Later, on the way home from dialysis, I start on the words again for practice.

"Si-si-bakwat. Yippee-ki-yi-yay. I'm going to remember to say that to Mom tomorrow. Yippee-ki-yi-yay."

Charlene looks at me, and I notice how wide her mouth is and how it turns down at the corners. Her maroon lips form a cupid's bow as distinct, though not as plump, as any of the buxom ladies in a comic strip. I read once, in a book on Chinese face reading, that a cupid-bow lip means an individual is proficient at getting what they want.

"I have to confess I told you a story," she says.

"A story?"

"You know what you said about a cowboy yell? Yippee-ki-yi-yay is just that, a cowboy yell."

"You mean it's not really an Ojibwe word?"

"No."

I laugh and change the subject, but inwardly I am amazed. Charlene laid out her lie as smoothly as the road ahead of us. And why? What reason could she have?

Maybe she didn't want to admit her ignorance of the Ojibwe language.

But she confessed, and that is admirable.

"I have a Bible," Charlene says, slipping the information adeptly into the conversation. "I read it sometimes."

I feel smug, remembering our last conversation about the Bible. What skill I must have shown, to change Charlene's mind so drastically during one conversation!

A week later, I drive her a third time. This will be our final dialysis trip together because I plan to quit the transit job and take classes to be a nurse's aide. I've never imagined myself pursuing a job like that. I did home care once, uncertified, and hated it. But in economically depressed Rusk County, CNA work has begun to look more and more attractive. At least I'll be guaranteed a job. Nursing homes are always looking for aides. Besides, my transit job has shown me that caring for people's needs is fulfilling. I have a hunger to do more.

The sun rises earlier now in May. Outside the car window, the sky lightens behind straight sticks of pines—row after row of them, with trunks like telephone poles—and fields appear, pale-eyed, like ghosts.

"Do you know what I marvel at in the Creator?" Charlene asks. "He makes everything in his creation round. The leaves are round. The sun is round. The drops of water. The scales on a fish. I can't think of one thing the Creator makes square. Even the blades of grass, when they first come up, are round, curled in a ball." Her face radiates delight, all the wrinkles together exclaiming.

"What's your idea of heaven?" she asks, as though she isn't satisfied with my answer from the first time. Probably she's only forgotten, but regardless, the question asked the second time holds the musky, lingering odor of a dare. *Go on. Get deeper. Tell me what you really think.*

"I get so tired of being trapped inside this body, this way of thinking," I say. "In heaven, I'll be free from this prison of myself. I'll be able to see."

"Hm." That satisfied thinking sound again.

Words that have bunched inside me rise to my lips. "All your life you've tried to serve God. Now you have one thing left to do before you die."

I have been thinking about this, worrying Charlene isn't ready to go. Normally, I would be scared to bring up the subject, but I know this part of Charlene, know if I appeal to her deep Native sense of the spiritual, she will be receptive. I want her to hear and understand, so I slow my voice and add depth to it, imagining myself an Indian, an observer of nature—and wise.

"In the Bible, Jesus told Nicodemus, 'Ye must be born again.' Have you ever been born again?"

"I don't know," Charlene says, her voice thoughtful, intrigued. "I've never heard that before."

"That story is in John 3. Do you want me to write the reference down for you, so you can go home and read it yourself?"

"Well ... I'll have to look for my Bible. I don't know where it is."

Oh. So whatever she told me about her Bible-reading habits, she hasn't read hers in a good long while.

I feel a twinge of anger toward all the churches Charlene attended without learning about the new birth—this thing I've been taught is the vital cornerstone of the Christian life. Not that I understand it myself. Not really.

I've always been taught that being born again happens at a certain moment when you ask Jesus into your life and

21

ask his forgiveness for sin. But Charlene, even though she doesn't know what it means to be born again, says she believes in Jesus. So is she a Christian?

I don't know.

I wait in the car while Charlene receives her dialysis treatment. Above the brown brick hospital, the sky stains itself pink and pale orange and makes me think of heaven. I think of Charlene's frail body and bright, interested face. I imagine her joy and excitement in a place that is bright and green and not stifled by pain. Small beneath the sunrise, I feel suddenly and deeply that the most important thing in the world is for Charlene to go to heaven. I want to meet her there to continue our friendship.

Most people have a dreariness they carry on their shoulders and in their eyes. Charlene, in spite of her frailty and pain, has a spark in her eyes that would startle a zombie to life. A woman like this is born for heaven, born for forever.

On the way home, I make my voice friendly and light as I say, "This is the last time I'll be your driver. Can I come visit you sometime?"

Charlene considers a long moment.

"Yes."

I am nine years old and lying in bed, afraid.

I have been afraid many nights before this and have learned to expect it. I will cry into my pillow, body heaving, clamping my mouth tight so that nothing escapes but a whimper. In the morning, I will be better. The sun will be shining, and it will be light outside, and I will forget. I will play in the sunshine with Lily, my lamb, and be happy.

But at night I am afraid.

I study the familiar lumps and shadows of my bedroom— the dresser, the big toy box, clothes and books and toys, the pale square of the window on the other side of the room. Downstairs, the door slams when Dad comes in from checking the cows, and then the house is quiet. My hair bun feels floppy and loose from playing all day. I can feel the strands of hair that straggle across my forehead and cheeks, and the hairpins that hold the bun in place are poking into the back of my head. I roll onto my side and push my hair behind my ears, trying to get comfortable.

Familiar words pop into my head: *where the worm dieth not, and the fire is not quenched*. I picture the preacher at revival meetings, standing behind the pulpit in his black suit, his voice heavy and his face passionate with appeal. I don't want to think about it. I want to go to sleep, but my mind is wide awake. I notice a shadow that is black against the wall, blacker than the darkness. I look at it closely, watch to see if it will move. It is nothing, of course, nothing at all, only my imagination.

What would it be like to go to hell? In my mind, I see orange flames licking, an endless expanse of fire below. I imagine myself there in the flames—though I cannot imagine the pain or the heat—burning and falling. Men are there with hard, angry faces, twisted in pain. They are all falling too, with the sea of orange separating them, and heat and smoke and white worms inside them that do not die. Forever and ever and ever falling because hell does not have a bottom to it. How could you keep falling forever? How could you not get to the bottom sometime?

My cheek is hot against the pillow. I flip it to its cool side and pull the blanket out from the end of the bed so I can stick out my feet. The shadow against the wall looms black, and I think I see shadowy fingers, reaching. It is only your imagination, I tell myself. I pull my feet back under the blanket.

What if I die tonight? I can't imagine dying, but what if I do? People do, sometimes. I remember a movie I saw once, about people who'd almost died, and had seen hell, and then come back.

"We don't know if we'll be here tomorrow," the revival meeting preacher had said. "God can take us anytime. If you died today, would you be ready?"

I don't know if I would be ready. I know that to go to heaven one must have an experience with God and be born again. But how does one become born again?

I can't go ask Mom and Dad. They think I am a Christian already. I remember a long time ago, when I was six, and Dora and Jennie asked Jesus to come into their hearts.

"I want to ask Jesus into my heart too," I told Mom.

"Do you hear him knocking on your heart's door?" Mom asked.

I listened very carefully and thought I heard a faint tapping inside. "Yes."

24

So now I am a Christian, and even wear a covering on my head. But how can that count if I didn't really understand back then?

Tears—the ones I knew would come—leak from my eyes and roll down my cheeks as a sob heaves up from my chest. I hold my body stiff and straight, keep the sound tight inside so Dora and Jennie won't hear from their bedrooms down the hallway. I release the air in a long, shuddering breath—concentrate on breathing in, releasing air, breathing in, releasing air.

"Don't let me die tonight, God. Please don't let me die tonight. Help me, God. I don't know what to do."

It could really happen. You don't really think it could happen, but what if it does? What if you spend forever and ever and ever in hell?

I've been afraid before, but always when I wake up in the morning and see the sun shining outside the window, everything is better. Tonight is different. Tonight, I am tired of being afraid and, for the first time, know clearly in my mind what to do. Because tonight is only one night, but forever is a long time.

I swing my feet over the side of the bed, find a Kleenex, and blow my nose. It won't be so bad, really. I can do it.

Quietly, so Dora and Jennie won't hear, I walk past their bedrooms and down the stairs, stepping on the back part of each stair so it won't squeak. Past the door at the foot of the stairs, with its dark window and the shape of a man behind it. But I'm not thinking of that now. I walk through the kitchen, with the clock going "tock-tock-tock" very loudly on the wall, then on through the library and the office, feeling my way past the vague, shadowy shapes of the bookshelves and Mom's sewing desk.

There is their bedroom door, a long white rectangle in the darkness with a thin line of light shining at the bottom. I can feel my heart beating in my chest. I raise my hand and knock.

"Come in," Mom's gentle night voice says. I push open the door.

The lamp is shining against blue walls. Their room is a clutter of things, like it always is. Hairpins and coverings and socks and a blue glass bowl on the dresser and books piled up on the shelves of the headboard behind the bed. Mom is in her nightgown, sitting on the edge of the bed with her dark hair hanging behind her. Dad is lying across the bed in his pants and white T-shirt, reading. They look up—pleasant, warm, not as scary as I imagined.

"I'm afraid if I die, I'll go to hell," I say, and burst into tears.

"You won't go to hell, not as long as you believe in Jesus," says Mom.

I feel better, just hearing her voice. I go over and sit on the bed between them, looking down and trying to gulp in the tears.

Dad lays his book face-down on the bed. "The Bible says, 'If thou shalt confess with thy mouth the Lord Jesus, and shalt believe in thine heart that God hath raised him from the dead, thou shalt be saved.' That's all it takes, Luci."

His voice is reasonable, confident. My tears slow down, and I listen, concentrating, to what he is saying. He reaches behind him and picks up his Bible—the black one with a brown spot worn into the front cover—and shows me the verse.

"Do you believe Jesus died for you and rose again?"

I nod.

"That's all God asks. Here's another good verse, in 1 John 1:9. 'If we confess our sins, he is faithful and just to forgive us our sins, and to cleanse us from all unrighteousness.' If you believe in Jesus, all you need to do is ask God to forgive your sins, and he will."

"You can say a little prayer," Mom says.

"Yes," says Dad. "Just say a little prayer like, 'Dear God, forgive me for my sins and take me to heaven when I die.' Then, you don't need to be afraid."

"That's all I need to do?"

"That's all. God doesn't tell us anything besides that."

Relief fills me.

"Let me write down the references for you, so you can read them. That's what I do when I'm doubting." He reaches behind him and feels around behind the stacks of books. "Honey, do you have a pen?"

Mom finds a pen on her nightstand, and an old envelope. Dad writes down the references in his funny, spiky handwriting and hands it to me.

"Thanks." I stand.

Mom gives me a hug. "Good night, love you."

"Good night, love you."

My body floats up the stairs and into bed. The pillow is cool under my cheek. I snuggle into the blanket, feel its softness envelop me. I lay the paper next to me on the nightstand and stare up at the ceiling.

"Dear God, please forgive me for my sins, and please take me to heaven when I die. In Jesus's name, amen."

God is very close. It feels as though he is right next to me, all around me, and above me. He must love me. People say that a lot, in Sunday school and church, but now, for the first time, I realize it is true. My insides are still and very joyful, and I cry some more, because it is so much.

"I never knew it was so easy, God. Thank you for saving me. Thank you. Thank you."

I feel myself smiling in the dark and fall asleep that way.

When I wake in the morning, I jump out of bed and go out to feed Lily. Carrying a dirty five-gallon bucket of water across the green lawn with the blue sky above me, I sing at the top of my voice, happier than I have ever been in my life. So this is what it means to be born again. I remember all the stories I have heard. It really does happen.

I think I will be happy forever.

One Sunday afternoon, a couple of weeks after our final dialysis trip, I visit Charlene. The lawn in front of her house is fresh green, and her maple tree has dropped winged seeds across the cement walkway and flower garden ... if it is a flower garden. I recognize empty tulip stalks and bloom-gone hyacinths, but the rest of the plants massed against the house and spread around the roots of the Japanese maple are weedy green things like you'd see in a roadside ditch.

I knock on the door and hear the little dog, Nibaa Ikwe, barking furiously inside. I wait, the moment long, conscious of myself within the strangeness of the moment, noticing things that do not matter—my feet on the cement stair, the bumpy grain of the cement, the splintered lines of the painted door. I pray for courage.

"Nibaa! Be quiet!"

The door opens and there is Charlene—small, a little stooped, and wearing a pullover too big for her body. She smiles, her wrinkles turning upward en masse.

I relax, and the moment normalizes.

Inside, the unfamiliar acridness of cigarette smoke pierces my nose. I think of cancer and try to breathe shallowly. We stand in the kitchen, a small room dominated by a round oak table beside a window overlooking the yard and driveway. The table holds various neat stacks of papers and paraphernalia and a green glass ashtray pushed to one side. From the tan-carpeted living room, a Native American bust regards me, grave-faced, from a stand. Two feathery owls perch on a shelf, and a miniature totem pole, painted with anguished Indian faces, rises beneath the living room window.

"Have a chair," Charlene says.

She sits down at the table and I sit across from her, not feeling shy anymore. Charlene is too tiny, too wrinkled, and too intensely present in the moment for me to remember to be shy. We talk as naturally as old friends.

She speaks much, and fiercely, of the evil American government, unchanged in greed and corruption since the day they fleeced the Indians. I think the government couldn't possibly be that bad and is at least better than some, but I humor her and agree.

We move on to talk of the wickedness of the world, and here I stand on familiar ground. I have no *real* experience with wickedness. I am only parroting what I've been taught and what I hear on the news, but Charlene speaks with real conviction. I know the difference instinctively. She talks as only a person can who's been hurt and is angry.

I hold in my mind that moment outside the brown brick hospital and steer the conversation toward Jesus.

"We are all so sinful, and I'm so thankful we have Jesus to be our Savior. What would we do without him? We'd be lost."

Charlene agrees wholeheartedly. "When I think of the woman who anointed his feet and wiped them with her hair, I can't imagine how she felt." Her eyes shine. "Can you imagine? I'm not worthy to kiss his big toe!"

She is passionate. She is simple. She touches me in a way not many people can. I—who am always watching, always analyzing, always separating myself from my own emotions and making fun of them—admire this capacity of Charlene's not only to have an emotion, but to become that emotion with every vibrating cell of her body.

"Did you find your Bible?" I make my voice casual, as though this is only a conversation piece, mentioned as easily as the weather or the traffic today.

"I'll have to look for it," Charlene says.

She stands slowly and takes careful steps across the kitchen to the door beside the stove. Nibaa follows her and crouches, body trembling with excitement. Charlene turns the knob with one hand and with the fist of the other rams the door with all her small strength. The door opens hard, wood scraping wood, and Nibaa leaps at it, barking wildly.

I follow Charlene into the room—a sort of storage and guest room with a bed in the corner. Boxes and oxygen canisters line the walls. There is a desk stacked with a jewelry box, stereo, and dozens of CDs, with a bookshelf opposite.

Charlene scans the titles on the bookshelf and shakes her head. "No, I guess it's not here."

"I want to give you a Bible," I say, eagerly. "Can I?"

She nods.

"I brought one, just in case."

I pulled it off a shelf in my family's bookstore right before I came. The bookstore—a room Dad built in the back of our garage—isn't a business so much as a community service, making just enough money to support itself, its customers sporadic and mostly Mennonite.

I hurry to my car and bring in the hardcover pew Bible I chose for her, its chief assets large print and a low price.

Back home, though, I regret that cheap pew Bible. When I visit Charlene a week later, I bring a second Bible, this time the nicest we have: black bonded leather, translucent gold-edged pages, and the words of Christ in red.

"This is to replace the other Bible I gave you. I just grabbed that one right before I came, but I want to give you this one instead."

When she nods, I open the cover and fill out the blanks on the presentation page.

To: Charlene
From: your friend, Luci
Date: July 3, 2011

Charlene looks at it thoughtfully. "I read books," she says. "They move forward. They have a story. But the Bible ... I think it would take something to get me to read the Bible."

She sets it on the stack of papers on her table, and every time I visit after that, it is in exactly the same spot, as though it hasn't moved.

A few days later, Charlene calls me. Each of her words across the telephone comes slow and distinct, potent with importance. "I need your help."

"What do you need?"

"My sister Mary had foot surgery, and her garden needs weeded, and she can't do it. I want to help her, but I can't do it alone. Would you be able to come tomorrow morning and help me weed her garden?"

"What time were you thinking?"

"It would have to be early. When the sun comes out, I'm done for the day."

I think of the camping trip I've planned with friends from church. I'll have to skip it if I help her, but I don't want to tell her no. I remember her frail body, the straight line of her back as she shuffled her way to my car. She wouldn't ask for help unless she really needed it. I feel honored to be asked.

We leave at sunrise, Charlene driving her long-nosed, full-bodied car—the kind I think of as an old person's car—with its power smooth engine and tan leather seats. Nibaa wiggles between us on the seat, and I hold her collar to keep her still. She is radiant and panting, her nails scrabbling against smooth leather, a doggy smell in her fur. I feel dirty, touching her in the contained space of the car. At home, dogs are farm animals who stay outside.

"I didn't know who else to call," Charlene says. "You're my only friend, besides Nibaa here." She smiles, pointed chin intent just above the steering wheel, like a little girl driving a house. "Notice I put you before Nibaa."

It seems to me a rare thing to be called the friend of Charlene. There is something fierce about her—something elusive and untamed and snappish—and I feel as privileged as if a wolf, ears twitching, brambles caught in its thick fur, has crept out of the bushes and gently licked my hand.

"Mary's got that big garden, and now with her bad foot can't do anything, so she's feeling pretty down. I want to teach her by my example." Charlene's fingers, wrapped around the steering wheel, are perhaps the most capable part of her frail body: slim, toned in purple, cool-dry, confident.

"I thought if she could see how I keep going in spite of everything ... I love her so much, Luci." Although her words are quiet, they vibrate with emotion. "Good, bad, or indifferent, I love her."

Mary's house stands at the end of a long, winding lane, surrounded with woods, a well-manicured lawn, a horse pasture, and a collection of shiny vehicles. As instructed, I open the car door and watch Nibaa take off in a heart-wild dash for the woods. Hobbling across the lawn with Charlene holding my elbow, dragging the garden cart behind me, I feel all the guilt of a trespasser. I don't think these people knew we were coming. They will wake up and look out the window and wonder what Charlene is doing with some Mennonite girl out in their garden.

Oh, well.

It is Charlene I care about.

I set the four-wheeled garden cart beside a row as Charlene instructs, and watch as she sits down on it and stoops to pluck a weed. While I weed one row after another, the weeds lifting easily from the soft dirt, she scoots herself forward along her row, painstakingly pulling a weed and following it, after a rest period, with another. After two hours, she has finished only one side of one row. Her fortitude and slow patience amaze me. At that pace, I would go insane. The woman's spirit is indomitable.

I sing as I work, choosing hymns and making my voice soft and beautiful. Maybe Charlene will be touched by the words, maybe she will think: *So this is what makes Luci so different and so happy. Because she has God in her life.*

"We'll weed the rows first, and then we'll get the spaces in between the rows," Charlene announces into my singing, her voice sounding brusque and businesslike. "The creeping charley are taking over this garden, and I don't think a tiller will get rid of them. We need to root out every weed."

I stop my song, feeling foolish. So Charlene isn't being touched.

We weed in silence. Nibaa sniffles up, her small body vibrating, and props sandy paws against the garden cart where Charlene sits.

"Git!"

Nibaa gallops off across the yard.

When the sun is hot and high in the sky, Charlene says she had better get out of it. "I'll come back another morning to finish."

"I can come and help you." Too bad she's so picky, or we would be finished already, but still ... I want to help.

Halfway back to the car, I put the garden cart down to let her sit and rest.

A Siberian Husky woofs from a kennel across the yard, and Nibaa strains against the leash in my hands.

"That's Adam's dog," Charlene says. She's talked about Adam before. He's Mary's son, the favored nephew who mows Charlene's lawn, who visits his paralyzed father in the nursing home, who is smart and steady and kind.

"Would you be allowed to marry someone who's not a Mennonite?" she asks.

I get that question a lot—from a blonde-haired girl I sit beside on a plane, from an old man I drive to a doctor's appointment, from a trim young intellectual in a business suit. It always makes me feel foolish and a little resentful. I don't mind the question, but why do they ask if I'm "allowed" to do something that can only be my decision? "Allowed" puts me in the category of someone who is under the control of someone else, like a child or a cult member or a pet.

Still, there's enough validity in the question to make it difficult to answer. If I married someone who doesn't practice in the way we believe to be biblical, my church wouldn't sanction the wedding. My parents and close friends would feel heartbroken and disillusioned. They would pray for me and weep for me and wonder where they failed. Girls who marry outside our circles are the ones who want to cut their hair and wear skinny jeans, not the ones who want to stay Anabaptist.

But how can you explain an entire worldview in a few simple sentences to an old woman who has no idea of it?

"I would want to marry a Christian," I say.

"I didn't say he wasn't a Christian."

"Well, to me the most important thing in the world is to know Jesus and to follow what he tells us in the Bible. And not all Christians follow the Bible the way my parents taught me. I want to marry a guy who follows the Bible, whether he's a Mennonite or not."

"Adam doesn't drink at all. Well, he might have a drink or two if he's at a family gathering. But that's it."

It amuses me that she doesn't see the chasm between our worlds. As if Adam would want a weird-looking Mennonite girl. Still, the idea pleases me. I like to be thought of as normal, a typical American girl who just might fall in love with Adam. I don't tell Charlene any different.

On the way home, Charlene complains about Indianhead's overpriced transport to dialysis. She had it out with the director, she says, and got nowhere.

"I can't afford it! Now that summer's here and the roads are good, I'm going to start driving myself once a week on Saturdays."

I think of the hour's drive to the Barron dialysis unit and of how tired and weak Charlene always grows when she's finished a treatment.

"You can't do that. What if you have an accident?"

"Then I'll be dead."

"What about when winter comes?" I am thinking now of the icy roads. "Will you stop driving yourself then?"

"Yes."

"Like maybe in November you'll stop?"

"Yes."

I doubt Indianhead is overcharging. They're a government-subsidized company, after all. But I do not doubt Charlene is destitute. I mull an idea over in my head until we arrive back to her house, knowing my tendency to jump good-heartedly into things without thinking ahead.

But this will be just for the summer, I appease my wiser self. Just on Saturdays, and I'll take my writing along.

I help Charlene out of the car and escort her into her house, examining my idea one more time to be sure it is sound. Just inside the door, I make my announcement.

"I can drive you Saturdays."

Her face bursts into light, wrinkles massing upward. "We can take my car, then it won't cost you any gas."

The following Saturday, sitting in the passenger's seat of her long tan car on the way to dialysis, Charlene looks at me, her face radiant.

"Why did you offer to drive me?" Her eyes are big with wonder, her words weighty with importance.

Because Jesus loves me, and I want to show that love to you. The words spring into my mind, but I could never bring myself to say something like that. It would sound cheesy and condescending, like a Sunday school story.

"Because you're my friend, and I would worry about you driving yourself."

The words come out lame instead of genuine.

Charlene's face drops and the light leaves her eyes. I wish I had given her my real reason.

Like all reasons for all things, my reason began in long-ago synapses and layers of memory, long before I tried to squash it down to a sentence and hand it to Charlene.

In one of those memories from the recently past winter, I sit on a weather-beaten board of the deserted, thrice-collapsed building down the road and past the woods from our farm. The sky is the washed-out color of winter, as though the blue has been run through the washer too many times, and the dye has leaked out. The cold is in my nostrils, but my body is cocooned with layers of sweatpants and socks and boots. The firmness of boards beneath me, my body hunched forward and arms huddled, boots hollowed into snow.

Twix, the three-legged farm dog, rubs against me sniffing and begging, and I run my fingers through the long fur at the ruff of her neck.

You know, maybe there really isn't a God. I have considered this possibility multiple times before, ever since I've been old enough to think and to question. I don't know when the questions began, but it seems as though they've always been there. Probably it's the words that have done it.

As long as I can remember, I've eaten words. Like a spider, I've dangled myself from long strings of words found in books into other worlds and other lives. Suspended between worlds, I have questioned the differences in how people think, questioned religions, and questioned God.

TURTLE HEART

People say that intelligence is a blessing, and that questioning and wondering about things is good, but I know they are wrong. People were not made to question and wonder. They were made to follow each other blindly, like pigs—to eat and sleep and grunt and be happy. I have ended up on the wrong side of the equation.

This time, though, the questions are larger, and the possibility of a world without God seems close to absolute. The world empties itself around me. I wonder what I will live for if I don't believe in God.

The questions are larger this time because of my creative writing class. More specifically, because of my creative writing professor. I am auditing the writing class at the nearest university, an hour's drive from home, and entering the unknown, sharply-pressed college world to learn about writing feels radical and scary. I observe the professor from my seat at the back of the class, aware of the power I have in silent observation, aware that he is aware of me, the only Mennonite student he has had, a girl, shy and pretty.

I have always known how to appease teachers, how to watch with bright eyes and a look of intelligence, how to give the answers the textbooks want. This teacher, though, fascinates me. He loves words, and I watch him talk and move his hands with enthusiasm while he talks. I have never met someone who loves words the way I do, who writes into them and exalts them and lives in them.

I had thought, listening to other teachers and other classes, that the love words had to be locked away, that the real words must be formulated and professional and sold to a market. This man does not say so. He does not say much of anything, really, only that words are freedom and meant to be free. He questions instead of answers. For me, accustomed to analyzing smug-faced people full up to their necks with opinion, the questions are disconcerting and powerful.

I begin to wonder—really to wonder—if there is a God. This man, I think, doesn't believe there is, or at least he isn't sure. Anyway, not the God I know.

I scroll through online journals that are part of our class assignment and read words cold, beautiful, haunting, the words of people who are in pain, angry, skeptical, disillusioned. Their words are so different from the smug, safe reading I am used to.

I wonder about these people whose lives are cursed with unhappiness, whose words wander and empty. I wonder about my creative writing professor who doesn't believe in God. If everything I have been taught is true—and I read the words over in the Bible, to see if they are there—then my professor, whom I love, and all these unhappy and cursed people who don't know Christ will go to hell, will step from one pain into greater pain and burn there forever.

I cannot accept that.

This is what causes me to question, really question, the reality of God. Oh, sure, there is evolution. I have read books of evidence for a Creator. And there is the Bible itself, attacked and refuted on all sides. I have read books of evidence for the Bible too.

But these things were only child's play, things I wrapped my mind around to employ it. Evolution or a nebulous Bible have never caused me to question God down in the deep places of my heart where change is possible.

Hell does.

I know, with a deep and burning hatred, that hell is wrong and that any God who would send people to hell is despicable and merciless.

Quite simply, I hate him.

I lie in bed for weeks—I don't know how long, but it feels like weeks—my mind numb, staring at the ceiling or sleeping.

I have always loved God ever since I was tiny. I loved him when I was nine years old and prayed to him in fear and felt peace envelop me. I loved him when I was older and homesick and felt his nearness as close as a wedding band around my heart. I loved him when I dedicated my life to him—recklessly, joyfully—at a public service.

Without God, I feel my life is not worth living.

With my doubt, I betray him who was my friend.

Two things finally pull me from this endless circling of the drain.

One, after staring at the washed-out winter sky and knowing the reality of no God, I realize something. I do believe in him. Way down at the bottom, where reason doesn't matter and where I don't know anything, not really, I believe in God. It is a tiny seed that I have not planted and cannot uproot. The belief doesn't have as much to do with evidence as it has to do with need. And that is all.

Walking home on the flattened snow of the country road, cold sharp in my nostrils, I pray the prayer Mary prayed with baby Jesus in her womb. "My soul doth magnify the Lord, And my spirit hath rejoiced in God my Savior."

I love him, I think. And I trust him. If someone is wrong, it is me, not him. Whatever he does, I trust him. Because he is good, and because he is God.

I am cradled in love, cradled like the baby Jesus in the womb.

At home, I start reading the New Testament, and this is the second thing that saves me. For a week, I do little else. By the fourth day, I have made it to Ephesians, and somehow, the simple reading of the words breaks open my heart. They speak to me like they never have before and maybe never will again. I am hungry, drinking them in.

By the time the week is over, my doubt is almost past. It still surfaces occasionally, and I still spend long periods of time staring into space and thinking. But mostly, I am happy. I drive for Indianhead. I start writing a book. And I take note of the changes in me. My relationship with God has stretched and deepened. I am more willing to trust him for the things I don't understand, and I have obtained an aching for people's souls that stretches my heart and makes it throb. For weeks, the aching consumes me, powers my tears and my prayers. I love them, every one of these beautiful people. More than anything, I do not want them to go to hell.

I tell Charlene, "I wanted to be an Indian when I was little," the following Saturday on our dialysis trip. "I would slip around the house in my bare feet, trying to walk silently and saying things like, 'Me Indian chief. Uh-hug.'"

My younger sister Kathy and I had our own teepee—really the refurbished metal cone from the top of the old grain bin. Dad cut a door into the cone, and he and Mom painted it white and decorated it with colorful symbols of moons and stars and buffalo. Kathy and I spent hours playing in that teepee, Kathy the squaw, cooking our meat, and me the Indian brave, sliding through the forest with my bow and arrow. We frequently went on the warpath, whooping it up, our hands slapping our mouths while we yelled.

"Well," Charlene says when I tell her this, "I bet you would enjoy the powwow up on the rez."

Enjoy it? The very word stirs my blood. I envision drums and dancing and Indians in feathers and war paint.

But I also worry. What if they make incantations to the spirits? Charlene has told me the Native Americans believe every tree and rock has a spirit, and she keeps sacred tobacco in her home from the funerals of dead relatives. I never want to be caught worshipping any spirit but the Great Spirit.

"Will I feel comfortable there?" I ask.

Charlene doesn't catch my meaning.

"Oh, yes," she smiles. "There are many pink skins who attend."

The Ojibwe reservation, Lac Courte Oreilles, is about an hour north of Ladysmith in a barren part of the country chiefly populated by deer and pine.

"What does Lac Courte Oreilles mean?" I ask.

"Lake of the Short Ears," Charlene says. "The French called the Indians 'short ears' because they didn't have any lobes on their ears. Like mine." She points at her own ears, short and flat against the side of her head.

We pay ten dollars for admission pins and wander through booths displaying T-shirts and bone knives and imitation arrowheads. Charlene holds her cane in one hand and the crook of my elbow in the other, which sometimes becomes awkward as we sidestep our way up narrow grass aisles between tables. Carved wooden pens. Soapstone animals. Signs. Bumper stickers. Beaded moccasins. Exorbitant prices.

I pay too much for two pieces of fry bread and the sodas to go with them, and we sit outside the dance circle eating and balancing the fry bread on greasy paper plates on our laps. I watch the professional dancers in feathers and fox skins and find them disappointing. Their moves are polished, but lack the primitive urgency of war, of bitter cold, of blood iced in deer prints. On the chairs closest to the dance circle, a group of tan-skinned, full-featured men watch, their bellies pushing out their tank tops and pudgy arms exposed.

I remember Charlene's anger that Ojibwe children weren't allowed to speak their own language in schools when she was a child and wonder if the culture she wants so badly to hang on to has been altered, not by white men's rules, but by doughnuts and plastic toys.

The drumming though. The drumming holds an echo of the ancient.

"If the drums don't have power," Charlene said before we left this morning, "why do they change the rhythm of my heart?"

"They change the rhythm of your heart?"

"My heartbeat is irregular, but when I hear the drums, my heart beats in time with them."

The drum sits, full bellied and tight breasted, next to the dance circle, a ring of Native men around it—T-shirted, tattooed, some swarthy, some pudgy—drumsticks slapping hide-leather surface in unison, wails rising.

A deep-voiced deejay announces that veterans will now be honored and asks those who are able of the audience to stand. I wonder, frantically, if I should stand and feel relieved to see that Charlene remains sitting. She will think I am sitting in deference to her.

Men, some in uniform, some in blue jeans, and some in feathers, step onto the grassy oval of the dance circle and begin to dance-march around it in a peculiar two-step shuffle. Most of the audience is standing now. Charlene looks at me, puzzled, and then, apparently deciding I need encouragement, shrugs and stands herself.

I sit, embarrassed, holding my body still so as to go unnoticed, hoping people will think I am sitting because I'm a clueless Mennonite confused about proper procedure, trying to pin an honor-the-veterans-while-sitting sort of look on my face, hoping above all things no one will guess the reason I am sitting—because I don't want to honor the veterans.

Charlene looks down at me with a sort of bright, interested look in her eye I would describe as intrigued. At least she isn't embarrassed to be seen with me.

TURTLE HEART

I am in a mega church in a southern state. The church, where I have come to hear a well-known speaker, is unlike any I've seen before. In my mind, it's fashioned more along the lines of an indoor amusement center than a church, complete with a coffee shop and Noah's-Ark-themed daycare.

A soldier on leave from Iraq is to be baptized during the service in a great pool high on a stage in a corner of the huge auditorium. The congregation is asked to stand, to let their padded, maroon, movie theater chairs flip up behind them while they honor his work as a soldier. And I, not wanting to sit while a thousand others stand, stand also, and think how incongruous it is for a church that professes to follow Christ—who died for every Iraqi soldier—to honor a profession which sets out to kill those same soldiers.

I regret my cowardice in standing.

And now, at the powwow, I regret my rudeness in sitting, refusing to honor the men who have done what is to them, and is to me, a noble thing. They have risked their lives while I live safe in this country.

It's just that the pennant of nobility my ancestors handed to me is different.

According to Martin family legend, my great-grandpa of ten generations ago spent time in a Swiss jail cell rather than recant his religious beliefs. Although we don't know for certain when or for how long he was jailed, we know that in 1732, he and his wife Elizabeth disembarked from the *Pink Plaisance* in the city of Philadelphia, where they were to join their sons who had already emigrated. "Christo Martin, age sixty-three," the captain wrote in the ship's log upon arrival, and our ancestor signed his mark—a circle and a vertical line—beside it.

Christian and Elizabeth, along with many other Anabaptists of Europe who had been harassed and discriminated against for decades, were drawn to the colony called Pennsylvania where a Quaker man, William Penn, had implemented a thing completely unknown in Western society: separation of church and government with the freedom to worship as one chose.

In the small Mennonite school I attended as a child, I learned about William Penn and his city called "Brotherly Love." I also learned how he'd treated the Native Americans with kindness, fairness, and respect rather than the dominant spirit so many other white men showed. And I learned how Pennsylvania had gained peace and prosperity as a result.

My dad's ancestors were Amish stock—I grew up hearing him speak Pennsylvania Dutch with my Grandma Miller—and it was an Amish man, Jacob Hochstetler, who had an encounter with the Indians we still talk about today.

Jacob woke one night in 1757 to a cry of pain from one of his sons. He found his son had been shot in the leg. Through the cabin window into the darkness, he glimpsed Indians and three French scouts lurking by the bake oven. His two other sons ran for their guns.

"No!" Jacob cried. "Don't shoot! The Bible says we must not kill."

"But Papa! We have to save our lives."

"No, boys. We must love our enemies. We can't shoot."

And so Jacob Hochstetler hid in the cellar with his family while their cabin burned to the ground. He watched his wife, daughter, and Jacob Jr. brutally murdered, and he was taken captive with his two remaining sons without lifting a finger in self-defense.

He escaped his captors seven months later, and his sons—who had been adopted and kindly treated by Indian families, with whom they maintained lifelong friendships—were released in the years that followed and reunited with their father.

And this, says the Amish man and the Mennonite, this is nobility.

The veteran's walk over at last, the deejay announces the dance circle is now open to anyone. Walkers of all shapes and skin colors stroll and dip around it, some in T-shirts, some in bright bought costumes, walking through the sharp heavy beat and the chant songs of the drums.

"You should walk the circle," Charlene says.

I shake my head no. I waver when she asks a second time but shake my head again. I would like to, but I am suspicious of meanings. Sure, it all looks motley and harmless, but didn't the long-ago Indians dance to ward off evil spirits or to call down rain?

Charlene leaves my side, makes her way slowly around the circle of onlookers and disappears. I finish my soda, watching the walkers. Scrunch my greasy paper plate in half and put it in the nearest trash bin.

"Luci Miller." The deejay's voice booms across the loudspeaker. "Luci Miller, come on down and join the circle of dancers."

I jump, startled. They don't mean me, do they? My heartbeat quickens. I spot Charlene standing next to the deejay. So that's where she went. I am frantic with confusion and self-consciousness, trying to decide. If I wasn't conscious of my little white cap and long dress among all the T-shirts and feathers, if those weren't TV cameras over there, panning the dance circle ... I back away, shaking my head.

During the hour's drive home, I don't mention the fact that I didn't walk. Charlene doesn't mention it either.

It's nice to know that in some ways she is as shy as me.

We talk about other things as nightfall deepens around us.

"I don't like Black people," Charlene announces, somewhere within the conversation. She glances at me to gauge my reaction.

"Why?"

She shrugs. "I just don't. They live on welfare, and they don't get married, and they pop out all kinds of little brats that the grandmas have to take care of, because the moms don't."

I feel my face heat, but my voice remains calm. "Your niece isn't married," I point out, "and she has a daughter, and her grandma takes care of her. And all your relatives on the reservation live off money from the government."

Charlene nods. "That's true. But I still don't like 'em."

My anger rises. So this is what this old lady who claims to love God has hidden inside her! Hate, pure and simple. This must be what the Bible means when it says the heart is deceitful and desperately wicked.

"Well, then you're directly disobeying God's command," I say, my voice heated. "The Bible says, 'He who loves God loves his brother also.' When you die and stand before God and you don't love your brother, how do you expect him to let you into heaven?"

Charlene looks pleased, her face smiling inside itself. I've become interesting to her, the vehemence unexpected.

"Well, I don't care if it is going against God's command," she says, after a pause. "I just don't like 'em."

Every Saturday after dialysis, we go to Taco John's. Charlene always orders the same thing—two hard-shelled tacos, no hot sauce, extra sour cream. She takes the first taco to our table right away—always the same table, nearest the door—and sends me back for the second after she finishes the first.

I always copy her order for myself. I would like to try something different, but Charlene always insists on paying. Since hard-shelled tacos are the cheapest, I order those.

"My sister Mary is getting together with the family at Josie Park," she tells me during one of our Taco John meals. "Would you want to come over for an hour or two this evening?"

My good intentions have started to feel a little worn after driving her all these summer Saturdays. Getting up in the dark, realizing hospital waiting rooms are not conducive to writing creativity, and falling asleep Saturday after Saturday on slippery hard hospital furniture has begun to take its toll on me. I've started to resent, just a little, her glad acceptance of my generosity. Now I wonder if she wants me to meet her family, or if she just needs a driver. Breaking into the family party of complete strangers is not exactly my idea of a fun evening.

Charlene's face remains bland and her voice casual, but her tiny body, draped in a sweatshirt, seems expectant, tense.

I can never resist her.

"Sure," I say. "That sounds like fun."

I pick her up later, and we drive out to Josie Park where her family sits grouped around a fire ring. Walking toward them, I expect them to turn with smiles, with welcome and questions and introductions, as my family would. When they do not, when they let me sit next to Charlene on a picnic table bench with only a brief greeting from Mary as welcome, I wonder if they resent my coming, and I feel foolish for being here. I watch them talk and eat and move around the fire, zoning myself away from them into the private watchful world of public places.

"Help yourself to the food," Mary says, and I am grateful.

Eating gives me something to do with my hands and awkward eyes. Charlene points out the members of her family—a couple of her brothers and their wives, Mary's husband, Mary's sons and grandkids.

Mary's husband, Ron, picks a beer for himself from the ice-filled cooler.

"Did you want a beer?" he asks me.

I laugh, used to my long dress and head covering eliciting teasing comments from well-meaning folks. This Ron is a quiet man, polite, but he must be a tease like a neighbor of ours. Only afterward do I realize he is serious. These people don't know the Mennonites any more than they know the platypus from Australia. I am in uncharted territory.

The family doesn't quite know how to treat a Mennonite. One of the sisters-in-law, a large lady with glasses and a balding head, says "Hell" once and gasps audibly. She glances over at me, her hand over her mouth.

Charlene is unusually vivacious. She tells the story of how I ran over a rabbit on the way to dialysis, and how, a few minutes later, I caught a sparrow in the grill.

"When I came out of dialysis, the sparrow was gone. Then I saw it in a bush by the door." She laughs and bumps my shoulder. "Hiding the evidence."

This is not normal. We are not the sort of friends who laugh and bump shoulders, but I chuckle as though I find it funny instead of annoying.

"Bloodthirsty," I say, an inane comment I regret immediately afterward, because it makes no sense.

Darkness falls, and with it, mosquitoes. Mary offers Charlene and me camp chairs next to the fire. I put my head back and close my eyes, trying to blend personality into chair. Act relaxed, and people will accept you better.

"We should get out the roasting sticks," somebody says.

From the grins passed around, I conclude there must be a joke about the roasting sticks.

One of the married sons, the one with the buzzed head, keeps laughing, looking at me, and shaking his head. "I don't think we should."

And then I see why. There are two wrought-iron roasting sticks. One has the shape of a woman carved onto its end with two sharp metal pokers protruding where her breasts would be. The other has the shape of a man with one poker in place of his privates.

Adults think this is funny? I sit and grin at the shock of it—not the shock of the pokers, but the shock of adults who laugh at the pokers.

"Do you want to roast a marshmallow?" Mary asks.

"Sure," I say. I hold my roasting stick over the flame, trying to look natural and unconcerned, as though I don't notice the fact that I am roasting a marshmallow on a lady's breasts.

This shock is familiar—world smash world, thud of impact, reverberation.

I am sitting again in creative writing at the university, distinctly uncomfortable while the class discusses

Hemingway's "Hills Like White Elephants." There is nothing in the story to make me uncomfortable, nothing except the fact it alludes to an unknown something which the teacher wants us to discern.

There is a marriage in the story, a relationship. I am desperately anxious that the unknown has to do with sex, afraid it is some mysterious yet basic part of sex everyone knows but me and that in the class discussion I will expose my ignorance. My face, so much more communicative than my mouth, has become my betrayer, eyes darting and bashful, color rising in my cheeks. Good thing I'm sitting at the back where no one can see me but the teacher. I know he is puzzled by my unease, and, of course, I cannot explain.

In this larger world outside my home, I don't know how to navigate. It seems to me that out here all people think about is sex, and all people talk about is sex. Even their swear words are sex words. Growing up, my people never talked much about sex, except to caution carefulness and purity. What I know is pulled from discreet comments, from women's conversations, and from half-felt things in books. I worry there are things—basic, important things—that everyone knows but me. Out here, I am all child, all three-year-old, with no smug barrier of knowledge to protect me.

What a relief to find that "Hills Like White Elephants" is a story about an abortion, not sex.

One day, Charlene gets out her photo album, and I sit beside her at the kitchen table, paging through. The childhood pictures first. They came in odd shapes and sizes, in perfect squares and rough-edged rectangles, sepia tones on stiff yellowed paper. I see Charlene: a beaming four-year-old with new dress and shoes, a six-year-old with missing teeth, a girl deep-eyed and dark-curled at her first communion, a twelve-year-old with long, thick braids. I study the twelve-year-old longest, recognizing the broad eyebrows with their scattered hairs, the eyes that are cautious and a little slanted, the wide, downturned mouth, and the tiny mole on the left cheek. The depth of the child's eyes and the clear thought of her face indicate ... something.

Unfulfilled promise, maybe.

The old lady I know is clever and sharp and funny, but a deep purple anger swirls just beneath her skin. I wonder what happened to the promise in the child's eyes—the delicate unfolding of petals, the mystery like soft skin.

Charlene, in spite of her professed love for her family, seems constantly at odds with them. She is always critical toward someone, always making blunt and unkind statements that drive them away.

Apparently, she can't control her temper ... but there's something else, something too nebulous for me to define clearly. It's almost as if she invites conflict to punish herself. She seems to expect alienation and even cling to it.

I remember something she told me once: "I had to do things when I was twelve no young girl should have to do." She worked like a man on her grandfather's farm and told me the story of her first harvest, when she was ten.

She was dusty and sweaty by the time the day was over, moisture lining the insides of her jeans, her thin shirt clinging to her back. The men—her grandpa, her dad, a neighbor man, and two of her brothers—were leisurely and relaxed, watering horses, unhooking harnesses.

"Let's have a beer," her grandpa said.

Grandpa was strict and practical and, unlike her dad who drank often, drank only once a year at harvest time. It was an honor for Charlene to take the beer from his hand, an honor to stand with the men and feel the camaraderie of a hard job completed, an honor to take the acridness and yeasty stink into her mouth for the very first time and know she had earned it.

"You never married? Never had children?"

She shakes her head. "No."

"You would have made a good mom," I say, almost believing it.

She shows me a picture of her Ojibwe great-grandmother and tells me how when she was old, she'd spent all her time looking for her boys. She would wander around the house, calling their names, and once—even though she was a tiny lady—pulled out the refrigerator to look behind it. After that, her daughter thought she shouldn't be left alone and put her in the nursing home in town. At the nursing home, Great-Grandmother refused to stay in bed at night and would wander up and down the halls, looking for her boys. The aides began tying her to the bed, but even the restraints couldn't keep her down. She'd work herself free and wander the halls again.

Charlene would be like that. She's the sort of person you couldn't keep in a restraint, the sort of person who would refuse to look at airplanes.

She turns a page in the photo album to her mother and father's memorial cards, dark with references to purgatory. They were Catholic back in the day when Catholics talked about purgatory.

Next, big-bearded Ollie, her youngest brother who died of cancer.

T.J., her great-nephew, who lived up on the rez, as Charlene always calls the Lac Oreilles reservation, and was murdered in a scenario involving drugs and a girlfriend.

John, the brother who made her young life miserable with teasing. "I love him, but I just don't like him," Charlene says.

Roxie, a beloved niece who died of an aneurysm that shot to her brain. The family blamed Charlene because of circumstances beyond her control. "I wouldn't admit it to them," she says, "but I blamed myself." My heart pangs for her.

Sue, short-haired and smiling. "My girlfriend," Charlene says. They must have been close. Sue is the only one of Charlene's friends to be honored in the family photo album.

Another page holds a picture of Ginny, one of her seven sisters. Charlene has placed a news-clipping, an obituary, and a memorial card beside her picture. I scan the clipping. It tells the story of a trailer home, a drug seizure, and an arrest. She'd put it all right there in the photo album with the smiling nieces and nephews, the new babies, the reunions, and the weddings.

Ginny worked as a prostitute in California, Charlene explains. When her liver failed, she came to stay with her family in Wisconsin. When Charlene met her at the airport, her face was as yellow as a California peach. Charlene cared for her and fed her and bought her this little mint-shuttered house on Lindoo Avenue. Ginny lived here until Charlene caught her drinking again and kicked her out. It was nighttime and raining and Ginny wondered where she would go. "You figure it out," Charlene said.

We page to the end of the album, and I watch children's faces mature from photo to photo. Charlene has them organized by families and knows exactly where each one fits—the children by a first marriage, the children by a second marriage, and the children by a boyfriend.

I didn't realize before that normal, middle-class Americans lived like this. I didn't know the entire structure of a family could be continually fluctuating, with divorce and separation running through it like a fault line. I didn't know that murder and drugs could be put in a family photo album, that they could be mentioned without shock and tears, or that they could be as much a part of somebody's life as cancer or breaking a leg.

We page to the end of the album, and a heaviness settles in my chest. I am glad to tell her goodbye, glad to leave the smoky house and drive down the road in the clear air, to walk into a sunlit kitchen and see Dad and Mom at the table with butter and bread and broccoli and soup spread in an untidy cluster in front of them, glad most of all to see them look up and greet me with welcoming smiles.

I make a practice of giving Charlene a half-hug after every visit, my arm encircling her shoulder while she sits in her chair.

But one day she's had enough. When I tell her goodbye and move in for a side-hug, she plants herself in the middle of the kitchen floor and holds her arms wide. "Now this is what I call a hug," she says.

The hugs become a tradition with us.

After dialysis one Saturday, after she's told me all about her sister Mary's problems, her face dragged down with worry, I want her to know I care. "I love you and I'm praying for you," I say when I hug her good-bye.

I don't expect Charlene's reaction. The worry drops from her face, her eyes light up, and her wrinkles repeat themselves in a thousand smiles.

I feel as though I've just saved the world.

"I wonder who I could get to wash my car," she says a few days later. "I can't do it anymore."

We sit side by side on the cement stoop of her house—her straight as a stick, me leaning forward, elbows on knees, letting hot summer sun drain into the pale underside of my arms. I smirk inwardly at the idea of Charlene's pampered town car needing washed. Her vehicle sits in the garage six days out of the week. My own Ford Focus, parked in her driveway, shows off its dusty sides admirably.

My family lives on a gravel road, and every time I come to town, I drive down that road, rocks popping from tires and dust flying. I never wash my car, considering it a waste of time and money unless, perhaps, I'm going to a wedding. Charlene's car most definitely does not need to be washed.

But this is her world, not mine. I've pushed aside the coats at the back of the wardrobe to crunch through unfamiliar snow. Charlene trudges toward me over the snow, head bent, alone, and more than anything, I want to reach her.

"I can wash your car for you," I say.

It won't take long. An hour or two, tops.

I arrive at her house at nine that Monday morning. Charlene looks up from her place at the kitchen table and stubs out her cigarette as I enter. Nibaa barks wildly and jumps against my leg, begging for attention.

I plunge into action. "Should I go ahead and back the car out of the garage? Where do you want me to start?"

"Just a minute. Slow down." Charlene considers, her lined face impassive, conferring this decision all the weight of a world war. "I think we need to go through the carwash first."

Apparently, when she said, "wash the car," she meant I'd be doing everything else but washing the car.

First, we take the car through the carwash in town. Then, we drive up to the vacuum outside the carwash and Charlene gives me four quarters to drop in the slot so I can vacuum the inside.

After the vacuuming, we drive back to her house, where I meticulously clean the dash and leather interior with a soft cloth and shaving cream. I hope this will be the end of the job and I can go home, but no such luck.

"Now we're ready to wax it," Charlene says.

She explains in precise phrases exactly how one waxes a car while I listen, outwardly polite but inwardly groaning.

If I ever wax my car, I wax it in a car wash. There, you sit back in your seat and watch foamy soap and rainbow-colored gooey stuff run down your windows, listen to the hard wall of the pressure wash pass you once, twice, followed by the soft mist of the spot-free rinse, and then put your car in gear and creep out beneath the noise of the dryers, watching small round droplets scamper up your windshield like mice. Simple matter, a car wash.

Waxing a car with this old-fashioned, filmy white stuff is not so simple. First, you must buff the wax onto the car, taking care to work only one section at a time. Then, you wait for the white stuff to turn cloudy, and, finally, you rub—a long time—with a cloth.

While I work, Charlene watches from her little garden cart at the side of the garage and directs proceedings.

"My Dutch grandpa taught me how to think through things ahead of time and do them right," she tells me, her voice dropping into the momentous wisdom that is becoming familiar. "If you do it right the first time, you don't have to do it again. So that's what you can teach your children that my grandpa taught me."

If I were the type, I would roll my eyes. If I lived alone in a little house and watched TV by myself in the evenings, I'd be impressed. But living on a farm with five siblings besides myself—there used to be seven before Jennie got married and Dora started nursing school—I don't have time to worry about whether I do mundane tasks correctly. I just try to get them done.

As I rub, I wonder if now would be a good time to bring up the subject of my new job at the nursing home. With a full-time job, I really can't take her on those long dialysis drives every Saturday morning. It would be too much. Surely she'll understand.

"I got a job," I tell her, my smile stretching extra wide. "They hired me at the Rusk County Nursing Home to work full time on the evening shift. I put in my application online, and they called me the next day, so I guess they really need aides. It'll be good to have a regular job again." I open my mouth to tell her I won't be able to take her to dialysis anymore ... and pause.

She sits perched on the garden cart, her face still. I know she's waiting to hear the rest, expecting me to say I can no longer drive her, but the stillness of her face holds me back.

She reminds me of a baby bird, a new-feathered sparrow perched on its nest with its mouth open, tiny heart beating just below the skin.

"I'll still be able to drive you to dialysis," I hear myself say. "I work the p.m. shift, so I can drive you in the morning and still be back in time for work."

When I'm halfway through the waxing, hurrying faster now that I can see the end of it, Charlene says, "We should stop now and have some lunch."

"I'm fine. I'm really not hungry."

"Well, I can't go anymore until I get something to eat."

"You go ahead. I'll finish this."

Charlene pauses, her back straight as an arrow on the little garden cart. "I need you to drive me to the Back Door Café."

Ah.

I help her into my dusty, hail-pocked Ford, unlovely but useful, and drive to the Back Door, one of those grease joints locals love. Charlene and I have eaten here before. She knows Bill and Rose, the portly proprietors. Often, when we come here, they are sitting at the table closest to the cash register, eating with a few of their friends and calling greetings across the room to other friends who have wandered into the restaurant.

We sit at the table nearest the door. Charlene orders the roast pork sandwich and I the mushroom Swiss burger. We talk while we wait for our food, and one moment rivets itself in my mind—Charlene leaning across the table, eyes dark and unfathomable, voice intent. "I'm reading the Bible. And Luci, I don't know why."

"Oh, really?" I keep my voice light. "You been reading it quite a bit?"

She considers. "Well, I read from three different places every day. I read some in the Old Testament and some in the New Testament."

"Three different chapters, you mean?"

She nods.

I am shocked. I thought Charlene never touched that Bible.

Later, back in the garage, while Charlene perches on her garden cart and I stand on a stool to reach the roof of the car, I venture into the "born again" subject. After our restaurant conversation, I find it easier to bring a spiritual subject into the cool cement garage, right alongside the physical realities of sun, earth, and air.

I've been worrying over her spiritual state in my mind, wondering whether Charlene is a real Christian when she can't point to a moment of conversion. Now, I try to explain to her what it means to be born again, casing in careful words this Christian ideal that seems to me so elusive—changing an old heart, a dead, stunted thing, for a new one.

I think Charlene knows more about the concept of being born again than she first let on. She's spoken of the "born-again Christians" more than once, each time with a barely discernible touch of acerbity. "I think we are born again after we die," she said once.

"Yes, but it starts here on earth," I said.

"It's a supernatural event," I tell her now. I've heard Dad say this, and it seems important for her to know. "Like my dad, before he became a Christian, he was into all kinds of stuff, but when God brought him to the end of himself, and he saw what he would become, he decided he didn't want that. So he gave his life to God, and God changed him completely."

Charlene's eyes stay on me while I talk, watching me work, her face open and smiling.

I learned much of my concept of God from my dad. I've always been respectful and a little scared and deeply admiring of Dad, and that's how I feel about God.

In one of my memories, my family and I sit at the table on a Sunday evening after church, eating whatever everyone pulls from the cupboards and refrigerator—vanilla ice cream, peanut butter, bowls of cold cereal—when Dad starts talking about his past.

It is a subject he seldom mentions—a dark, fascinating place of rebellion, of beating his mom and being sent to foster homes and praying to Satan. We children are quiet, ears pricked like rabbits to catch every word.

"I was deranged," he says. "I took a mouse once and skinned it alive—everything but its feet and tail." My father! A peace lover, one of the ministers in our church, a man I know only as kind.

His eyes are black, regretful. "Some of those scars never really go away."

I have never seen that look before or since, not until I sit across from Charlene at the kitchen table one day.

"I did things when I was young I would never do now," she says. Her eyes are black, regretful.

Now and then, I tell Charlene I love her. She never says it back, but I don't mind. I say it because I think she needs someone to love her and to tell her that they do. I say it in the same light, friendly way I might say it to my mom at bedtime or one of my good friends when we wave goodbye. To me, saying "I love you," is a normal part of life.

But Charlene, when she says it, makes it abnormal. Earthshaking.

She sits across from me at the kitchen table one day, smoking. And I do what I would not do for anyone else— breathe in the smoke and become one with it, not wincing, not minding. It's all part of entering this mysterious thing called Charlene's world.

She stubs out her cigarette, lays it in the ashtray, and looks at me, her eyes dark and direct. "I love you," she says.

She does not look down as I would. Her eyes are naked. I can't bear it. I don't want someone to undress in front of me.

"More than anything, I want you to be happy. I am not like other people. When I love someone, I love them forever."

I feel caught and cheapened. My mouth has been uttering ancient mystical incantations of which I know nothing. I look for a reply and can't find one.

After a long silent moment in which I do nothing but smile, she lifts her chin and talks about other things.

By the time I get up to leave, I've formulated words that will have to do. Standing by the door, I hesitate, and then say, "I love you too. I'm not real good at putting things into words, but I do love you."

Charlene lifts her chin. "I can accept that."

At home, I pound my thoughts onto my laptop.

She told me she loved me, and it broke my heart to hear her say it, because she loves me freely and unreservedly and forever. It broke my heart. I think that is what the Bible calls agapé, and it does strange things to a person's soul. No one ever in all my life told me they loved me like that. She has an amazing amount of courage, that lady. That declaration of love did something to me ... it changed me. I didn't want to talk to anybody. I cried inside the rest of the day.

PART TWO—THE AWAKENING

One day her heart dropped out
and fell into my fingers.

SEPTEMBER 2011

Summer passes quickly, with me rising to meet two demanding tasks: my new job as a nurse's aide and the new and surprising responsibility of matching Charlene's love—that needy, trembling thing—look for look and throb for throb.

On a day in late September, I lie on my back in golden leaves, taking my supper break where I like it, alone and outside. The nursing home where I work overlooks the Flambeau River, and I like to sit on the slope of it and watch the ripples follow each other in their endless journey, the cars humming across the bridge a quarter mile away. Sitting alone, while the other aides take their breaks in the smoke shack or the cement-enclosed canteen downstairs, I feel secret and clever.

Today, I lie beneath the big maple tree, the old nunnery to my right and the river down the slope a ways. The air is as fresh as if it's been breathed from some far-off green mountain in Switzerland. I pluck my phone from the leaf-strewn grass beside me and dial Charlene's number, staring up through golden leaves at patches of periwinkle sky. She picks up on the fourth ring, and I imagine her tottering steps from the living room recliner to the phone stand in the kitchen.

"Hi, Charlene. This is Luci. I was wondering if you'd want to come over Monday morning for coffee and meet my mom and sisters. I have the day off."

Her voice vibrates across the line, warm and dark, the color of chocolate. "You don't know how good that makes me feel, Luci, that you want to spend your day off with me."

"I love spending time with you," I say, and consider, just a moment, my next words, wondering if they are true. But yes, they must be. My heart is warm with love, dancing with it. "You are the joy of my heart."

Mornings, before the pain catches up, are easiest for Charlene, so I pick her up at eight and drive out to our farm. Mom meets us at the door, her face circled in smiles. "So nice to meet you!" I see my mother as I think Charlene must see her—skin summer-tanned, nose wide, her dark hair sprinkled gently with white.

Silage is caught in the mat in front of our door, and the smell of manure drifts up from the barn, but when we step inside, the house is bright and cozy and smells like vanilla candle.

Charlene and I sit at the table with Mom and two of my sisters. We chat, and I watch Charlene's face grow animated, her words spicy. She refuses coffee but accepts half a muffin. She glows when the rest of us laugh at her jokes. She seems to have no intention of leaving for a very long time.

Like me, Charlene grew up on a farm, but she never experienced the pleasure or the humor or the close family connections that make a farmer's life bearable. From a young age and although slight of form, she worked like a man, filling in the gaps her grandparents left as they aged. She was to inherit the farm when she was sixteen and old enough to sign the papers and, for this reason, did not mind the work.

Then her grandparents' oldest daughter moved up from Chicago with her "wino" husband and two sons. She moved into Charlene's room while her husband and sons took the other upstairs bedrooms. Charlene had to move downstairs. She resented them from the beginning. Since her aunt had a job in town and since the boys were city boys and not much good with farm chores, her workload didn't lessen. While attending high school, she would do the morning chores, come in from the barn, make breakfast, and then walk the two and a half miles to school.

Just before Charlene turned sixteen, and when the temporary stay had lengthened to a permanent one, the aunt made a proposal to buy the farm. She and her father drove uptown to the register of deeds and transferred the property to her name. Although the farm had legally changed hands, the aunt never did get around to making the payments.

"At the age of sixteen and a half, I left," Charlene says, when she tells me the story.

"You left?"

"I just couldn't stand to watch my grandparents, who were my parents, deteriorate. You know, just getting old. And all the work I had to do ... If I wasn't working, my aunt found work for me to do."

Charlene moved into town to live with her sister Ina and Ina's two little girls. Ina's husband was off in the military, and their house was a shack with rotting timbers that allowed snow to blow into the bedroom at night. Charlene refused to sleep with the girls at first, because, when it was cold, they'd wet the bed instead of getting up to use the chamber pot. But as winter progressed and the weather dropped to twenty below, Charlene and the girls slept together just to stay warm.

"Did you still go to high school?" I ask.

"Oh, yes. I always went to school. I enjoyed school. It was a way to get away from everything. To relax."

"Did you have good friends there?"

She shrugs. "I made friends with the unpopular girls who weren't a part of any clique. I wanted them to have someone too."

She tells me about her first date during high school, with a boy from her class, and how he took her to the skating rink in town.

"That must have been fun."

She shrugs again. "I didn't find it all that exciting."

Charlene, it seems, never found guys exciting.

"I was engaged three times," she tells me. "One was a really nice guy, but I couldn't bring myself to marry him. I just couldn't find a guy good enough for me."

I think about that. "That sounds sorta conceited to say you could never find a guy good enough for you." I note her look of surprise, as though she's never considered such a thing as conceit. "But I know just what you mean. I never could find a guy good enough for me either. Except one ... and that never worked out."

I am nearly twenty-one when I meet Jake, having just moved to another state, where I teach grades one through four at a small Mennonite school. He is a sandy-haired teenager with a big grin, still in high school and four years younger than me. I notice how kind he is to the younger children—the students in my classroom—and admire his shy ways which seem to hide so much wisdom and emotion. I am sure he likes me. Even though we don't talk much, I *know* him with all the certainty that love brings.

Stretched in the spring lawn outside the schoolhouse one day—alone, drinking in the lushness of emerald and azure after the students and other teacher have gone—I realize I would follow Jake anywhere and do anything for him, if he only asked.

Sure, there've been other crushes, other intense flames of dream and desire ... but those were only imagination. This is real love, backed by clear-eyed, adult decision.

I write a letter to him in a small blue notebook, a letter both tentative and passionate, and hide it away under my dresser where no one will ever see it. I add more letters to the notebook during my three years of school teaching and carry them with me when I move back home to Wisconsin.

Now, a year and a half since I've lived near him, the flame of my love has cooled. I would still follow him anywhere, do anything for him if he asked, but he hasn't, and that's that. Dreams cannot digest air.

I haven't found anyone I like better and still reserve a place called hope in the back of my mind, but I think of him less often than I used to.

A few days after taking Charlene to meet my family, I go to her house early before work to take her grocery shopping.

After we've put all the groceries away and I am ready to step out her door, she stops me.

"I have a question for you. The other day when you said I was the joy of your heart, I thought about it and I thought, 'I don't go to church with Luci. I don't sing with Luci. I drink and smoke and cuss. Luci must not be very particular about her friends.'" She smiles a little saying it, puts a lilt in her voice, and I understand the effort to make a serious thing casual.

"Charlene!" I stare at the floor, smiling and shy, searching for words.

She keeps on. "I love you too. Every morning when I pray to the Lord, I say, 'Thank you for Luci.'" Her eyes touch me directly, her voice low, warm, and intense. "You have become my inspiration for living."

"Thank you, Charlene."

I leave, shaken. Her eyes hurt me, the way they are dark and deep and look straight at me. And the wrinkles that move with her eyes, up or down or deepening ... they hurt me too. I could not be so vulnerable.

She is wrong in what she says about herself. I've never seen her drink or heard her cuss. That's all in her past. And who could blame her for smoking? It's not her fault—it's an addiction. She doesn't understand her worthiness, her value that reaches deeper than any jagged shards from her past.

I drive toward the post office to mail a couple of letters.

Next time, I'll explain to her why I love her. I'll mention it next time.

Nervousness flutters in my stomach. There is a reserve in me that dislikes talking intimately with anyone. But Charlene needs to know her worth, and now is not the time for cowardice.

It's still early. Maybe I can go back and tell her before work.

I look up to see a sign that says, "Do Not Enter," and realize I've pulled up to the post office from the wrong direction.

"Cripes."

I wonder if that's a bad word.

I stretch across the passenger's seat, trying to reach the mailbox that's on the wrong side of the car because of my mistake. I drop one piece of mail and it flutters to the ground outside the far window.

Oh, criminal.

But this playing with "swear words" is only a cover, a flurry of distraction while my deeper brain considers Charlene's needs.

I'll go back and talk to her, I decide, jumping out to retrieve the letter. A car pulls up to mine, nose to nose—from the right direction—and I scramble to get inside again and to back out onto the street.

Sometimes in life you must make yourself do something just because it's the right thing to do.

"I mailed the letters," I say, standing just inside the door.

Charlene, sitting at the table, stubs out her cigarette and looks at me, puzzled.

"I still had a few minutes before work, so I stopped back to tell you why I love you so much." I sit across from her and lean my arms on the tabletop. Nibaa nudges my knee, but I ignore her. I gather the words and set them in front of Charlene as loud and straight as I am able, saying them slowly and making them count.

"You are one of the bravest people I know. You are one of the least complaining people I know. You are precious to God, and you're precious to me. You are one of the most honest people I know. When you love, you love unreservedly, and that is a beautiful thing to do. You have an interesting mind. I love talking to you, and I love that you listen to me."

Her face is blank. Open. "You know, Luci, in all my seventy years, no one has ever said these things to me before."

"Well, they should have. They're true."

She nods.

I hug her goodbye, feeling I have done the right thing. Mission accomplished.

When we see each other again, Charlene says, "Luci, I was thinking ... if you wrote down all those things you told me, maybe when I was missing you, I could read them, and it would help me."

At home on my next free afternoon, I write the words on college-lined notebook paper as well as I can remember them and, inspired, add more.

I miss you when I'm away from you. I pray for you when I wake up in the morning and when I go to bed at night and lots of times in between. I will always be your friend. Always. It doesn't matter what you've done in the past or what you'll do in the future. I love you. I love you exactly the way you are, for the person you are. I love your spiciness and your opinionated-ness and your smallness. I love your dark eyes, a little slanted and deep as two wells in a midnight wood. I love the way all your wrinkles turn up and your eyes lighten when you are pleased about something. I love your smile. I have never seen anyone look as joyful as you when you smile. I love your voice and I love the dignified way you have of expressing yourself. I love your original expressions like "ding-dang" and "burrrr-ito." I love your straight Indian nose and the tiny mole at the tip of it.

Your body is frail, but your spirit is large and wide as the sky. I know that you will probably leave me before I leave you, and I cry inside sometimes, thinking about it. I have never lost anyone I really loved before. But one thing I know is you believe in and trust the same Jesus I believe in and trust. We may have different backgrounds, different demons, different lives, but we both trust in that same Jesus. The Jesus who said, "Lo, I am with you always, even to the end of the world." The Jesus who said, "I go to prepare a place for you. And if I go and prepare a place for you, I will come again, and receive you unto myself; that where I am, there ye may be also."

When we meet in the place Jesus has prepared for us, your legs will be young and strong. There will be no more doubts, no more questions, no fears, no pain, no crying, "for the former things have passed away." And we shall see his face, and his name shall be in our foreheads, and we will have all of eternity to know him and to love him, to live and to explore and to praise him with our lives.

Amen. Even so come, Lord Jesus.

Your friend who loves you with all her heart,
Luci

Charlene places the letter on the end table next to her recliner, tucking it beneath the doily. I find it there once when I am dusting. "I've read it so many times I almost have it memorized," she tells me.

On one of my days off, I take Charlene to Lac Courte Oreilles to pick up her prescriptions at the reservation pharmacy. After the pharmacy, we stop at the Smoke Shop, where she buys twenty packs of cigarettes, and then, closer to home, we stop at a roadside restaurant where we order hamburgers and fries and talk about modesty.

Charlene asks why I wear dresses.

"Because the Bible says women should dress modestly, and wearing a cape dress like mine"—I show her how it's sewed with an extra layer of material over the bodice—"helps to set a standard of modesty."

She looks skeptical. "I don't see why you can show your arms but not your legs."

"I do show my legs. I wear flip-flops."

"That's your feet, not your legs."

I see her point. "Well, do you want me to start wearing long sleeves on all my dresses?" I ask, unreasonably.

She studies me, tilting her head. "My family was a lot different than yours. There were fourteen of us kids, and the girls shared a bedroom with the boys. We never thought about modesty."

She picks up her hamburger in that careful way she has and takes a bite, chewing slowly. I have seen her face— impassive behind her small, rimless glasses—spark without warning into joy, spitefulness, sorrow.

"You know, you remind me of my sister Kathy," I tell her. "Her face is expressive, like yours. I like expressive people."

She nods.

"Do you think my face is easy to read?" I ask.

She looks at me thoughtfully and shakes her head. "Not really. You have three expressions I've seen. There's your Luci expression—"

"What's that?"

"That's what you have on your face right now. When you're just smiling and being Luci. There's your shy expression. And there's the expression you have when you talk about God and Jesus." She shakes her head. "I can't describe it. It looks like you're going to fold your hands and rise up to heaven."

Really? I didn't know what I felt about God showed on my face.

I remember her words from several days ago: "All my life I have taken care of my brothers and sisters because that is the purpose the Creator has for me. And now I wonder if his purpose is different than I thought, if there's something more I need to do." Her eyes were blank and soft, wondering.

I thought she was talking about religion, about being a messenger to her brothers and sisters. She wants what I have because I am happy and kind and gentle and talk about God like a friend, and she wants her brothers and sisters to have it too. Her bony little hands are trembling for this, reaching ... but I don't know how to give it to her. I've tried.

"Don't you want to ask Jesus into your heart?" I asked her once.

"He's already there," she said.

"How do you know?"

"Because he's always been there."

I will try again, will phrase the question differently this time.

I wait until we're back on the road, collecting my nerve and praying. Finally, I look over at Charlene. "You know what you said about the expression on my face when I talk about God and Jesus? That makes me happy because it must mean what I have with God is real, and people can tell." I let my uncertainty show in my voice, keeping my words hesitant and soft.

But her face signals agreement, and that gives me the confidence to ask, "Do you want that same sort of experience? Do you want to pray and ask God to take control of your life?"

She nods.

"I could pull over to the side of the road and pray with you."

She nods again.

On a quiet road between trees, I pull over. I've never done this before and don't know how. Shouldn't there be some sort of conversation about repentance? Or giving her life over to God? But I don't know how to talk about that.

"I'll pray first, and then you can pray," I tell her. Maybe she can take example from my prayer.

I close my eyes.

"Dear God, be with Charlene. Thank you for loving her so much and sending your Son to die for her. Lord, you know Charlene loves you and has tried all her life to serve you, but she hasn't had all the teaching that I have. But she wants you to take control of her life, Father. Please take her life and make her into your child. In Jesus's name, amen."

I wait.

Charlene is quiet, not praying. When I look over, I see that her eyes are open with unshed tears in them.

"Do you want to pray now?"

She shakes her head no.

"It's okay to cry. Crying is healing."

She shakes her head again, and the tears disappear, leaving her face lined and quiet. "I'm going to stop being angry with God for all the pain he gives me," she says, looking straight ahead, her voice low as though this is a form of a prayer. "That is wrong, and I'm going to stop being angry."

When she says no more, I put the car into gear and pull back onto the road.

"Do I have to tell people I'm born again now?" Charlene asks.

"No," I say.

Only later do I realize she was being sarcastic.

Over the next few days, I don't stop at Charlene's place before work as I often do. I need a break after the intensity of our last conversation, and I know I'll see her again Saturday when I drive her to dialysis.

Early Saturday morning, bright with sleep and anxious to see her, I let myself into the mint-shuttered house on Lindoo.

"Good morning!"

Charlene stands at the kitchen sink, her back toward the door. I expect her to turn, to see her face light up like the sun, and to hear a warm good morning in the voice she reserves for the people she loves.

But when she says "Good morning" the words are flat. She does not turn around.

I feel a twinge of disappointment. Well, maybe we've gotten to the stage of being "normal" friends now. We're moved into being casual and comfortable and taking each other for granted. No big deal.

But Charlene is on edge. When we arrive at the dialysis unit, she snaps at me for being stupid about the parking, and I snap back, regretting it later on the smooth, stiff waiting room couch. I want to show Charlene the love of Jesus, and here I am, snapping at her.

"I'm sorry for being grumpy," I say when dialysis is over, and I've helped her into the car again.

Her expression clears and opens. "When you didn't come to see me for four days, I thought maybe you would call. But you didn't call, and I thought, 'Maybe she's been in an accident and killed.' Those are just the little thoughts I have. And then I thought, 'Well, I think if she had been in an accident, my sister Mary would hear about it, and she'd tell me.'"

Seriously? After only four days? For the first time, I realize Charlene must wait for my visits, and I imagine her in her little house, waiting. I know she will look out the window sometimes, and smoke a cigarette, and give the dog something to eat, and sit down in her recliner and watch TV. And the day will be long.

"I'm sorry. I guess four days goes by like nothing for me, but for you, it's a long time."

She nods.

That evening, I sit at my desk in my upstairs bedroom in front of the window overlooking the yard, the gravel road, and the cornfield across the road. A fat autumn fly buzzes against the glass, and I watch it climb the window with its sickening spidery legs. From three pieces of paper, I cut three hearts in shades of red and pink, each heart slightly larger than the last. I glue their tops together so that you can lift each heart and see what is written beneath. "I have never felt myself so loved," I write on one of the hearts, "except by my mom." From my Bible, I copy out a verse from the Song of Solomon. "Set me as a seal upon thine heart, as a seal upon thine arm: for love is strong as death ... and the coals thereof are coals of fire, which hath a most vehement flame. ... If a man would give all the substance of his house for love, it would utterly be contemned."

The words are from a book of love letters, but I like the poetry of them. They fit the depth of my friendship with Charlene. Anyway, she won't know what the rest of the book is about.

Early the next morning, while the sun is still pink, I take the card to her house.

"I wanted to say I'm sorry for the way I hurt you."

"You didn't hurt me." She examines the card, smiling. "Well, this is precious. But aren't you up awfully early?"

"I wanted to surprise you and show you I meant it."

Sometimes I think I will choke on this friendship. It feels as thick as gooey marshmallow and hot chocolate in the bottom of the mug. The hugs have grown longer and longer, uncomfortably so, with Charlene rubbing and patting my back, but I never pull away first. I don't want her to feel rejected.

"I don't know why you love me," she's told me several times.

One day, I say the words back to her. "Why do you love me so much?"

I feel as though I gave a few drops of love and received an ocean in return, a tsunami that is sweeping me out to sea.

She stays quiet, her gaze sliding past me. She almost never looks directly at me when she talks. Instead, she looks down or to the side, as though direct eye contact with speech is too invasive.

"At first I had trouble accepting that a beautiful young girl like you loved me," she says, after a while.

It is the first and only time she's called me beautiful ... but I know she thinks it. Her eyes always watch me, drinking me like wine.

A few days later, she answers my question, slipping the words into an unrelated conversation. "I guess I have an ulterior motive for loving you so much. I wanted somebody to love me, so I thought if I loved you so much, you might love me back. And I was right, now you love me." She says it defiantly, as though making a confession.

I nod. So Charlene's love, which I make so much effort to meet, isn't all selfless admiration. It has purpose. But when

I think of the defiant way she said, "I wanted somebody to love me," my heart throbs.

I visit Charlene almost every day now. Besides the Saturday dialysis trips, I stop over before work to chat or spend a morning with her, vacuuming or helping in her flower garden or taking her grocery shopping. On days I don't visit, I call. Since my realization of her long days alone, I cannot bear to think of her lonely and missing me.

Still, the times spent with her have grown to be too much. I didn't realize, when I started, that one day of helping leads to the next and the next and the next ... and all of it takes time from the things I want to do, like the young adult novel I am writing.

"Would it be okay if I stop driving you to dialysis on Saturdays?" I ask one morning as I spoon lumpy balls of dough and raisins onto a cookie sheet. "It's just too much for me with my job and everything."

"I just need you one more month," she says. "If you could just get me through October."

And so we agree, with me relieved to have a deadline. One more month I can handle.

Charlene's birthday comes on a Friday, the twenty-eighth of October, and I invite her over for cake and ice cream. Mom and my sisters and I give her presents, and we all sing "Happy Birthday."

"I've never had such a shindig on my birthday before," she says.

"Really?"

"Never. When I was a girl, my aunt gave me underwear."

I work hard to make her day special, but inside, I am ready to explode. For the past month, I have eaten Charlene and drunk Charlene until Charlene leaks from my pores and dribbles out my nostrils. And she is eternally finding more things for me to do.

Just this morning, when I picked her up for the birthday party, she wanted to run a few errands. So we stopped at the bank, made her insurance payment, and picked up a few groceries, arriving at the party an hour later than planned. A few errands run at Charlene's pace inevitably turns into a couple of hours.

There seems to always be just one more thing to do until my time is gone. Lately, I've begun to wonder if the lonely old lady bit is an act she uses to manipulate me.

Today, I feel especially pressured because she's invited me to a family gathering for Sunday, and I told her I would go. The only problem: Sunday is my birthday, and I didn't realize, when I accepted Charlene's invitation, that Mom had already planned a meal and invited guests. Now I don't know which party to attend. I find it hard to tell Charlene no. She lives to see me.

On Saturday, I drive her to dialysis for the last time. She is peppy and joyful, probably looking forward to her family gathering tomorrow.

"I want to stop at my sister Mary's place on the way home," she tells me.

There goes more of my time. I've about reached the end of my patience.

"I won't be able to come to your family thing tomorrow after all," I say. "Mom planned a party for me."

Charlene pauses, then speaks slowly. "I thought to myself that was really something, that your mom would be willing to give you up on your birthday."

"I don't know why I have such a hard time telling you 'no,'" I say, darkly. "People like you run right over me."

I've never said anything unkind to her before.

Her face, which had been alight with happiness, flattens, the wrinkles dead. When I start to turn down the road to Mary's house, she shakes her head.

"No. Let's just go home."

On Monday, I stop in before work to apologize. "I was mad because I felt like you were taking advantage of me."

"Luci, if you don't want to do things for me, don't offer."

"I know." I grin, caught. "Were you really disappointed that I didn't come with you to meet more of your family?"

"So what if I was?"

"Then I have just one question for you. Why does it matter so much?" I've been thinking about this, trying to understand. I was glad to have her meet my family, but I wouldn't have been disappointed if she hadn't. There must be a reason this is important to Charlene. Maybe she wants me to witness to her family about Christ.

"Luci," she says, "if you don't know why, I can't explain it to you."

I feel justly condemned.

She calls a few days later. "I wanted to tell you not to come over today. My nephew Jason was killed this morning in a head-on collision on the highway. I'm going to be with my sister."

In the week following her nephew's death, Charlene is quiet and abstracted. We go to the Back Door Café for lunch one day, and she doesn't talk. She only looks out the window onto the street, gathering words to tell me something that, in the end, she never says. At her house—sitting at the table, smoking cigarettes, watching the dog—she seems distracted, pondering whatever it is she holds in her mind.

She's sad because Jason died, I decide, and grow respectful and patient. She must be having a spiritual crisis. Maybe her nephew's death spoke to her, and she finally wants to become born again. I don't know how to define our prayer on the road together, but it doesn't seem like the kind of definite, transformative experience that counts as truly being born again.

On the day before Jason's memorial service, she turns from the window to look at me and finally voices her question. "Do you think it's wrong for me to love you the way I do?"

"What would be wrong about it?"

"You know, for a woman to love a woman like that. What you said the other week—why does it matter so much—do you think it's wrong for me to love you?"

I smile. Now I understand. Charlene's heard all this stuff about gay people on the news, and she's got it in her head that it might be wrong to love me as much as she does.

I never heard much about being gay before I started working at the nursing home. Until recently, the word "gay" was just a fun little word found in old readers: "Lighthearted and gay, Sally and John went out to play." Homosexuality was something my family and I would have been embarrassed to mention. If we talked about it at all, we might say it in a half whisper and hurry on. Probably because we don't have a television at home, and television is where such things become familiar.

Now, as my siblings and I grow older and connect more and more frequently to the larger world through the internet, all that is changing. My job at the nursing home also connects me to the larger world. I hear the word "gay" frequently, blared from multiple televisions in residents' rooms. Charlene is sweet to worry about this. Sort of innocent.

"I don't know what would be wrong with it," I tell her. "In the Bible, Ruth loved Naomi, and David loved Jonathan."

She smiles, all her wrinkles turning up. "I'm glad."

I've agreed to take her to Jason's funeral, and when I arrive at her house the next morning, she sits at the kitchen table. She's not smoking or playing solitaire as usual, just sitting. I sit across from her, the bright oak table with its stack of papers, the Bible, and the green glass ashtray between us.

"How are you?"

She shrugs. "So-so. I have a question for you. Just give me a yes or a no."

"Okay. What's your question?"

"Will you be my helpmeet?"

Her body, hidden beneath her bulky sweatshirt, is as tiny and crushable as a glass figure skater I saw in a storybook once, poised on a shelf with one leg uplifted. Her face as still as the fragile pink ice.

I remember how I told her once I would help her whenever she needed me, in whatever way she needed and, remembering that promise now, experience a form of helpless, tied-up anger. Charlene isn't going to let my promise stand on free will. She is working to bind me, and she'll bind me so tight I have no avenue of escape. I'll be tied to long days of helping and spending time in her small, smoky house, with her small, smoky, depressed, and angry self.

I feel sickened—as though something dead has moved close to me and tied itself to my skin—but resigned. I promised to be here for her, and I will. It's more important than anything because she needs me.

Charlene, her face tense, waits for my answer.

"Yes," I say.

Her face relaxes, wrinkles release. She is happy, but my stomach hurts.

We mince awkwardly to her car, her hand through the crook of my arm, and I help her onto the passenger's seat, pull down her seatbelt, and reach across to snap it in for her.

"I forgot my cigarettes," she says. "Would you get them for me? They're on the kitchen table."

I keep my face mute.

Not so long ago she told me, "You never give me a hard time about smoking like everyone else does, but you must think about it. It's a dirty habit, almost as bad as drinking, and I should stop."

"I didn't figure it would do any good anyway," I said, pleased with myself for refusing to nag, and with such positive results. I don't tell her how much I hate those cigarettes, how I view them as degradation and slavery and sin. I hate even to bring them out to the car for her because I feel it will be giving consent.

But I don't say that. Instead, I take the key she holds out and let myself inside the house, find the maroon ten-pack lying on the table, stuff them into the pocket of my leather jacket, and hurry back to the car, running a little—just for fun, and because she's waiting.

The atmosphere in the car is syrupy, making it hard to breathe. In the wake of her moving question, Charlene has become soft-spoken and conciliatory, not her usual passionate and opinionated self. I match her sweetness with sweetness of my own—even though it tastes like phlegm in the sides of my throat.

After an hour's drive—with me handling her car cautiously around the wooded curves and dark pine roads of the reservation—we arrive at the Lac Courte Oreilles community center where the memorial service will be held. We make our slow way inside, Charlene's arm through mine as she smiles and greets people. I smile too, and duck my head, shy. This is the first time I've come to a large-scale family gathering with her, and I am ashamed to be here, not knowing how to introduce myself or describe our relationship.

Strangely enough, I sense hesitancy even in brassy Charlene.

"Do you want me to introduce you to everyone?" she asks. I shrug, and she answers her own question. "Might as well not, there's too many to remember."

I sit in a corner, just behind Charlene, and watch the family move around the room in short-cut or long-swinging hair, in short black skirts or jeans, in earrings and bracelets and tattoos, and feel conspicuous with my unmarked skin, my long dress, and my little white cap. Like a saint or a nun … and who wants that when you are just turned twenty-five? I want to be young and free-spirited, not righteous. But I've grown used to this conspicuousness of dress and wear it like a security blanket. It's my identity, chosen for me before I was born.

People drift toward the circle of chairs at the center of the room, a Native drum in its center. I hang back until Charlene motions me to sit beside her.

She stands up suddenly. "Trade places with me. I won't sit where I have to look at *her* the whole time." Her voice is harsh and loud, a crow's raucous screech among a chatter of sparrows.

I obey automatically, wondering what she means. Then I notice Dinah, Charlene's sister-in-law—a short-haired woman with a pale face and parsimonious lips—sitting directly across the circle. Charlene has told me stories about this woman. I hope Dinah didn't hear her, but Charlene is talking loudly enough the whole room probably did.

I have always taken Charlene on her own terms, have rarely seen her interact with people in a social setting, and now I feel disappointed, disillusioned, and angry. This obnoxious, sharp-voiced little woman is my beloved Char?

A girl with necklaces, long wavy hair, and a peasant skirt gives an invocation in the Native tongue. She is white but married to one of Charlene's nephews and, Charlene whispers to me, the only one in the group who can speak Ojibwe.

A young man with long black hair lopes into the room and around the inside of the circle, soft-footed on the hard tile floor, holding something that smokes in his fingers.

"Burning sage," Charlene says, "to ward off evil spirits."

As he passes, she waves the smoke in toward her mouth and nostrils. "Aho." Her voice loud in the quiet circle of people. "Aho."

I sit stiff and uncomfortable, relieved to see a few others who do not wave in the smoke.

The long-haired man runs out and comes in again with the other drummers. They take their place around the drum in the center and begin their rapid drumming and their chant—voices meeting and escalating, dropping in tone, rising again, always together. The sound reverberates through the enclosed area, filling body and bones with wailing and rhythm.

After the drums and a time of sharing memories, men and boys move aside the circle of chairs and set up tables for the feast. They bring out dishes of food and set them down the sides of two long tables. This, Charlene tells me, honors the Ojibwe tradition of men preparing the food and women cleaning up afterward.

Someone announces that the elders should eat first, and the young ones should fill plates for them. Young people gather along the tables, filling their plates. I follow, filling a plate for Charlene. I want to do the polite thing, but afterward wonder uneasily if I have committed a faux pas. Maybe this practice of filling plates is a privilege only for Indians and not for strangers.

Charlene sits at a table to eat and calls me to sit beside her, but I shake my head. Someone else was sitting in that chair only a few minutes ago, and they might come back. Instead, I sit alone in a corner of the room and talk to a little girl. No one pays any attention to me, but I smile anyway and try to look as if I belong, as if I don't feel the hot shame and burning self-consciousness of being the outsider.

When we return to the car to leave, Charlene looks whipped, the lines of her face dead.

"Can you hand me a cigarette?"

I rummage in the car's side pocket where she usually keeps them, but the cigarettes are not there. I search—on the seat, on the dash, on the floor. No cigarettes.

Her face is tense, desperate.

I remember how I ran to the car, cigarettes stuffed into my pocket. They aren't there now.

"Didn't I give them to you?" I say, trying to wiggle out of blame.

"I don't know!"

I search the back seat. No cigarettes there either.

On the drive home, Charlene is like a sealed bottle of soda and vinegar. She makes pleasant conversation the entire time, but I can feel the grating in her voice, the hiding of how badly she wants that cigarette.

"So what did you think of the memorial service?" she asks.

"It was nice. I liked the drums. I wasn't sure if I did the right thing by getting you a plate. I thought afterward maybe that wasn't the right thing to do."

Charlene's answer is emphatic and warm. "You are a person who does whatever you want to do. You've shown that today."

She must mean because I didn't sit beside her at the table. I'm surprised that a seating choice made such an impression.

"Nobody could quite figure us out," she says. "They wondered what Char was doing ..." The words trail off, and I finish for her.

"They wondered what Char was doing with a Mennonite."

She nods and smiles.

"See what I go through for you?" I ask, grinning.

Aware of her tense body beside me, I speed most of the way home, pushing the car to seventy. We pull up in front of the garage in what seems a surprisingly short time.

"Can I have the key for the house?" Charlene asks.

I put my hand in the pocket of my leather jacket. No key. I feel around on the seat. "I thought I gave it to you."

I wait for the explosion—I have heard her sharp tongue aimed at others—but she doesn't say anything, just jumps out of the car and heads toward the house on her wobbly legs. I pull into the garage and look for the key, praying to find it.

Ah. There it is, on the passenger's side, pushed into the crack of the seat. At least she won't be able to blame me.

I get out of the car and see the missing pack of cigarettes lying on the garage floor, right beside the driver's door. I scoop them up and hurry toward the house, but Charlene is already inside, sitting at the table.

"How did you get in?"

"I had another key," she says, vaguely.

She is careful, now that the cigarettes are within reach, not to act hurried. She waits a bit before taking one from the pack, takes her time about lighting it, and slowly puts it to her mouth for the first puff.

"Thank you for not yelling at me about the cigarettes," I say.

"Shot happens." She smiles. "See how I cleaned that up for you?"

I laugh and turn to go. "Well, guess I'd better get going, or I'll be late for work."

She lays her cigarette on the ashtray and stands to hug me. "So what did you think of my family? Do you think you'll be able to live with us?"

I am taken aback at the words. Her attitude, the very air around her, still seems sickly sweet—but I rise to meet the occasion. "Yeah," I say, nodding and smiling.

"We're a wild bunch, but we have lots of love. I hope you sensed that."

I sensed nothing of the kind, but I am not thinking about that now. The words about living with her family have finally hit home.

I walk out the door mechanically, vomit in my gut.

Is that what this whole thing is then? A lesbian thing? Comments she's made click into place. *You are a person who does whatever you want to do. You've shown that today*. The reason she couldn't bring herself to marry. Her girlfriend, Sue, in the photo album. Her heartfelt question: *Is it wrong for me to love you the way I do?* and my idiotic reply.

Just what had I thought she meant when she asked me to be her helpmeet anyway? That term comes from the Bible.

"It is not good that the man should be alone," God had said. "I will make him an help meet for him." So he created Eve. Charlene knows that story as well as I.

It's just that I never envisioned her as a gay person.

I don't know many gay people, it is true, but from the bits and pieces I've heard—from a news article, maybe, or people's comments—I've formed a picture of them as angry, going around half naked or wearing transgender clothing, carrying signs to defend their rights.

I met a couple of gay men, briefly—one of them pleasant, aesthetic, long-haired, a dance teacher, and the other an old man who wears a kimono and carries a purse and has thin, arched eyebrows in a coarse male face. They fit the description I think gay should be. Charlene does not.

Then there was Lila, a large, talkative girl in my creative writing class. Smart, friendly, and opinionated, she was older than the fresh-out-of-school girls and made more of an effort to reach out to me. Once, when I was assigned to critique one of her pieces, she rescinded it before I'd even read it and submitted something she said I'd feel more comfortable reading. Skimming my eyes quickly over the abandoned writing—a passionate making of love between women—was the first I caught on to the fact she must be gay.

We were still friendly toward each other after that, but I thought she seemed a bit uneasy around me. Nothing you could put your finger on, but … something. I thought she felt guilty around me—proof in my mind that she knew what she was doing was wrong. I also thought she must be angry inside because her main characters were always angry, and her stories peppered with swear words. She disliked the Christian religion and was writing a fantasy about Death personified.

I thought gay people were angry at the world and angry at God.

But Charlene loves the Creator. She wears blue jeans, is hard hitting and straight shooting, and carries an aura of practicality about her. She holds her body with reserve, isn't lustful, isn't angry ... well, maybe angry.

But that she could be lesbian blows my mind.

I drive to the nursing home, my mind in a high heat. I have never felt so angry or humiliated in my life. I have to go back. I have to extricate myself from this humiliation as quickly as possible. I hustle through the steps of my job— passing linens down the long hallways, helping residents to the bathroom, scurrying to answer the monotonous, beeping call lights, pushing frantic words together as I work.

Supper break comes at four. I hurry out to my car, half running. When I walk in the door of her house with a brief knock, Charlene sits where I left her at the kitchen table. Her eyes light up when she sees me.

I sit down and drop my tote on the floor. "Charlene, what did you mean about me being your helpmeet?"

The light disappears from her eyes. "I wondered if you'd help me when I needed it."

I don't believe her.

"If you meant your helper and friend, I can be that. But I'm not your helpmeet like Adam and Eve were helpmeets." I work carefully away from the words "lesbian" and "gay." Such a thing is too embarrassing to mention. Besides, what if I'm wrong? "I'm not tied to you. If I meet a guy and fall in love, I might move away with him." I hope she understands my meaning.

"When you asked me that question, I thought you meant your helper and your friend. I can do that, but you said something when I left ... you said you hoped I could live with your family. I was glad to meet your family, but they're not my family. I'll always be your friend, but I'm not your person. I'm not your helpmeet in that kind of way."

Despite my anger, I keep my voice gentle and very kind. Deeper than my anger, I sense her fragility and do not have it in me to rail.

"Listen to me, Char. You are emotionally stronger than I am. You are more passionate and more intense. I find it hard to tell you 'no' because you sit there, and I see such need in your eyes, and I want to meet that need. But I need space. It's not in me to be that close to anyone, except maybe my husband if I ever get married."

Charlene sits quietly, listening to my words, her face defeated.

I wonder at my own gentleness. I've told people off in times of anger for offenses far less, and now, more affronted than I have ever been, I am only conscious of her vulnerability.

And I never thought I could look into someone's eyes and speak clearly on a subject fraught with such emotion. I'm fighting for my identity now, and that must make the difference.

She rallies with a comeback. "I was just thinking the other day, I don't know why Luci thinks I take advantage of her when she told me a long time ago she would dust for me, and she hasn't done it yet."

Her reply is so unexpected, it makes me laugh. "Yeah, I know. I didn't forget about it. I'll come tomorrow to do the dusting. I'll come early before work." I get up to leave and touch her shoulder as I pass. "I love you."

"I love you too," she says, quietly. I expected anger, and the words don't register.

"What?"

"I said I love you."

"Oh." And I am gone out the door.

Charlene again sits at the table when I arrive the next day. Her face is tight when I say hello, and she does not smile. She watches with barbed eyes as I pick up her animal figurines, one by one, to dust beneath them.

"Be careful!" she snaps when I bump one and it teeters on the shelf. I work my way around the corner into the living room, relieved to be out of sight.

"This is neat—this little Native American nativity set," I call. "I never noticed you had this before."

"Not very observant, hmmm?"

When I am almost finished dusting, she comes into the living room to sit in her recliner. I hear the vibrating hum of the oxygen concentrator starting up and turn to see her put the nosepiece carefully in place and hook the tubing around her ears.

"Did you notice where I hung your picture?"

She means the photo I gave her in a pretty, white frame. I noticed it hanging in her bedroom, directly across from the foot of her bed, when I went in there to dust. "Yes, I saw it."

"I hung it there so I could see it first thing when I wake up in the morning and go like this." She kisses her fingertips, and I smile, pleased at the compliment, until I see her fingers are still moving, swiping the air. "And give it a slap."

Her insult is so ingenious—so Charlene—I can't be offended. When I hug her goodbye, her tiny body remains stiff, her wrinkled face tight.

"You goofball," I murmur, feeling a burst of affection and empathy.

"You can call me names if you want." She is the epitome of hurt dignity.

I leave for work, but those final words bother me. I didn't mean to hurt her feelings. On my lunch break, I go back. This time, Charlene's eyes do not light up at the sight of me. She doesn't say anything but waits to hear me as though expecting to be slapped.

I sit on the footstool, close to her. "I'm sorry I called you a goofball. I wasn't trying to be mean. I meant it for nice, like the way I call you ridiculous sometimes."

Her face softens.

The next day, my day off, I worry about her and call on the phone. "I just called to say 'Hi' and to tell you I love you."

"I love you too," she says, her voice warm.

I stop in before work the next day, and she smiles vibrantly when I come in the door. Her brother and sister-in-law are there talking with her, but she reaches over and squeezes my hand. We share a long look. Friends again.

Still, I am suspicious, and I have nowhere to go with my suspicions.

If I ask, "Charlene, are you gay?" she could just as easily say no as not.

I don't ask.

Maybe the situation works on her mind too. One day, a few weeks later, she asks what I think about a news story on television.

I haven't heard the story, but apparently a football coach has been having sexual intercourse with some of the college boys he teaches. His fellow coach, an older man, knew for a long time what was going on but didn't report him, and now both men have lost their jobs and are going to jail.

"And he's an old man! Isn't that the most unjust thing you ever heard?" She is watching me, waiting to see how I respond.

I can feel the revulsion that enters my eyes and crawls across my face at the thought of what the coach did. "Well, what that coach was doing was a crime, wasn't it? The older man should have reported it."

Charlene's voice drops, and she looks away. "Yes, but I think it's terrible they would treat an old man like that who worked hard all his life." Her words lack their usual fire. She is only filling space.

She's feeling me out, I think. She wants to know what I think of homosexuals. And she's ashamed.

I am in creative writing class, this time a special session at a restaurant near the college. We are making up for several missed classes, sitting around a long table with drinks and a smorgasbord of appetizers, critiquing several of the students' works.

Lila's first. She has woven the beginnings of romance, an attraction between women, into her fantasy about death.

I can see the discomfort in the other students' faces as the discussion begins. They talk about the other parts of the story, no one willing to mention the obvious. I think it is partly because I am here—me with my long dress and prim covering and shy, sweet face.

Then it is my turn to talk, and the professor with his bland eyes looks at me, picking out the one scene that highlights a sense of attraction and asking what I see in it. Pinned down, I have to bring this thing into the open.

"She's trying to hide it, but she feels attracted to this ... this *person*."

I cannot bring myself to say woman.

Then I think the word came out sounding scornful—like a person is the next thing to a worm—and wonder if Lila noticed it. I wouldn't want to make her feel bad.

I wonder now, with Charlene, what it would be to have something I've done, something I *am*, too shameful for another person to say aloud. And she grew up in an age when most people thought like me. Her early years were very different from these modern years of easy acceptance and gay rights. She surely wouldn't have chosen her attractions.

I love her so much, I can feel every beat of her shame.

But I have no experience with gay people, no knowledge of them, and I question my own judgment. Maybe I took Charlene the wrong way. Maybe she isn't gay at all. While I debate, daylight grows shorter. Snow falls and deepens.

"If you're ever working, and there's a snowstorm," Charlene has told me several times, "remember, I have a guest room. If you need a place to sleep, I'll leave the door open, and it will warm up in no time."

A simple snowstorm—I've weathered dozens of them— would never deter me from my own warm bed and comfy pajamas if it wasn't Charlene who asked. Charlene, who is tiny and frail, who spends long days alone and glows with gladness whenever I visit, who has few people in the world who care about her. I think I detect a note of longing in her voice, and I want to make her happy. I make plans to sleep overnight in the guest room and to stay the following morning to help her with a few things.

I can read excitement in a certain stillness of her face and in the tenseness of her body.

"I'll have to find myself some pajamas," she says. "That guest room is so cold, you'll have to sleep in my bed where it's warmer. I usually sleep naked, and I know you don't want to sleep with a naked woman."

I have uneasy visions of Charlene lying in bed beside me, breathing in my nearness, blissful. I don't think she would try to have sex with me—but she might want it. The thought sickens me.

I talk to Mom about it. It's the first I've told anyone the embarrassing reality of my suspicions and the reasons for them. I beat around the bush a lot, adding many "ums" and "maybes" and "I don't knows," but Mom, who is used to my indecisiveness, understands.

"But I don't know for sure that she's gay," I say. "I don't want to sleep in her bed, but I don't know how to tell her that."

"Take an extra blanket and tell her you want to sleep in the guest room," Mom advises.

When I return to Charlene's house the next day, I pile blankets onto the living room floor with my backpack.

"What are those for?"

"I brought extra blankets so I can sleep in the guest room. You use an electric heating blanket, and I think your bed will get too warm for me."

"I only turn it on until the bed warms up, then it's off the rest of the night."

"Well, my room at home is cold, and I can sleep better in a cold room."

Charlene digests this information, her face disappointed.

"My younger sister always wants to sleep with me," I say, so she won't take the refusal personally, "but I never like sleeping with her either. I like to roll around and have the bed to myself."

"Well," she says, after a pause, "as long as you want to sleep in the guest room, we may as well open the door, so it can warm up in there."

Just before going to bed, I hear a commotion and then Charlene's angry voice, swearing at the dog. I am not fooled anymore into thinking she never cusses.

A moment of silence, then, "Luci!"

I hurry into her room. She sits on the edge of her big bed, naked except for her underwear, her legs dangling like two sticks—helpless and undignified. Her little brown belly pooches over the elastic band of her underwear. Even Charlene has a belly, I think, and after that am careful to keep my eyes only on her face.

"I took out my denture and put it right there"—she points at her bedside table—"and Nibaa ran up and grabbed it. And then she took and ran under the bed with it, because she knows I can't reach under there."

I hunker to the floor and peer beneath the bed. The denture lies on the carpet with Nibaa crouched beside it. I flatten my body and wriggle head and shoulders beneath the bed, reach for the denture, and wriggle back out.

"Here you go," I say, smiling, my eyes on her face.

"Thank you." Her lips slope inward toward her gums.

Funny. I've always admired her straight white teeth without realizing she wears dentures. I wash and brush old people's dentures every evening shift at the nursing home, but I've never put Charlene in that category. Frail and sick, yes, but, with her black hair and the vitality of her spirit, never old.

Two things keep me awake: the smoke and Nibaa.

I roll back and forth all night, hiding my face beneath the blanket, trying to block the smoke smell that permeates the small, cold room. At first, I think the smell must be old smoke, layered into the carpet and bedding, but it seems fresh and acrid, not stale. I finally go out to the kitchen and move the full ashtray from the cupboard to the table, where it's no longer in a direct line with the guest room door.

It helps, a little.

Nibaa, in a frenzy, trots excitedly from my room to Charlene's and back again, nosing up against my bed, her toenails clicking on the linoleum as she passes through the kitchen. She's about to drive me nuts.

Around two or three in the morning, she jumps onto the bed and curls up on top of the blankets in the curve of my legs. I never thought I would sleep with an animal, but I'm so relieved to have her finally quiet, I sleep in the same position all night, careful not to disturb her.

When I shift in the early morning, Nibaa jumps out of bed and trots back and forth from the guest room to the back door, asking to be let out. My eyes feel tired, and I have a headache from breathing smoke all night, but I know I'll never get back to sleep now. I slip my glasses on and follow Nibaa into the kitchen. My hair, taken down for sleep, swings light across my shoulders. Fine and soft, it has never been cut and tapers off in an uneven tail below my waist.

I clip Nibaa's leash onto her collar and let her outside, feeding the leash through the closed door. Charlene enters the kitchen behind me.

"Good morning!" Her voice sounds raw and deep, a smoker's morning voice.

"Good morning."

We smile at each other. She in a soft blue bathrobe, the lines of her face stark and her dark hair mussed, and me in my favorite mismatched pajamas from the thrift store.

I open the door to let Nibaa back inside, but in the process of doing her business, she's managed to wrap her leash around the five-gallon bucket Charlene keeps beneath the rain gutter. I slip into my boots and step down into the yard to untangle the leash, wondering if any neighbors are awake to see me in pajamas and hanging hair, and not caring if they do. This is the privilege of early morning.

I use the rail to pull myself onto the cement stoop from the side—a big step for my black-pajama-bottom legs—and flip my hair behind me.

Charlene watches and smiles, her flashing white dentures and sparkling eyes and every wrinkle on her face revealing joy.

She has seen me in pajamas, hair falling around my face, and thinks that I am beautiful.

I stay overnight once in a while after that. Not often, because I hate the smokiness of the house and because sometimes she gets upset and yells at me. I think a thin film of anger permeates the house like the yellow smoke on the walls. Staying there, I feel cut off from the world.

But I enjoy the early mornings when I stay over. Our ritual is always the same. I sit across from Charlene at the table, sipping a cup of rewarmed coffee, while she smokes a cigarette and plays two games of solitaire, head down, flipping the cards fast. "It gets my brain going," she tells me.

Then we read our Bibles together. Every day, Charlene reads from two different places in the Old Testament along with one chapter from the New Testament. She reads straight through, like she's reading a novel, finishing one chapter and flipping over to the next bookmarked spot so efficiently I wonder if she even comprehends the words. I read more slowly, trying to meditate, distracted by watching her.

Afterward, we talk, wandering into spiritual discussions the blatant business of afternoon would scare away. Charlene looks at me with such softness in her eyes at these times.

"Talking to you about God just makes me love you so much," she says once.

As she reads through Old Testament law, with its stonings and snake bites and inflexible judgments, her understanding and acceptance of those laws broadens my own understanding.

Always before, I viewed the laws as harsh and merciless and could not reconcile the Jesus of the New Testament with the thundering Elohim of the Old. Charlene views the laws as establishing justice.

"Why would God tell parents to stone their own son for rebellion?" I ask her. "That's just wrong."

"Well, if children saw that is what would happen to them if they rebelled, do you think there would be very many rebellious children?"

I have to concede she has a point.

Charlene loves two things on television: westerns and *Animal Planet*. Often when I stop to see her, she'll be watching *Animal Cops*, spitting mad. Maybe because of a man who let his horse die of malnutrition or one who chained his dog so tight that putrid flesh rings its neck. When the show explains how the individual was fined or had his animals taken away, she grows even angrier.

"They should chain him up without food for three days and see how he likes it. That would teach him a lesson."

I don't like her strident, cawing voice at these times. It makes me think of a witch. This harsh part of her character repels me. Not only has she no pity for evildoers, she has no sympathy for weakness or ineptitude. "If I had a deformed baby or one that was imperfect, I would take it out to the woods and give it back to the Creator," she says once. "That's what the Ojibwe did."

"You don't mean that," I say, chilled. "You wouldn't really do that."

"Yes, I would." The firmness in her voice leaves no doubt of her conviction.

One day she asks me, with real anger in her eyes, "Why does God let sinners live? Why doesn't he kill them immediately?"

Her harshness makes me defensive. "Then you would be dead too."

She nods and thought deepens in her eyes. "The wrong things people have done to me, I could have stopped at any time, so I was just as wrong." She is not recanting her view, only agreeing that if God followed the way of unrepentant justice, she also would be dead.

It seems an odd way to acknowledge wrongdoing, and I wonder why she phrased it that way: *the wrong things people have done to me ... so I was just as wrong.*

As winter progresses, Charlene develops a dry cough that leaves her struggling for breath. "Bronchitis," she tells me. "If there's any misery the Creator can throw at me, he will throw it."

One evening when I call her after a dialysis treatment, she doesn't answer the phone. I grow frantic with worry. She's always too sick after a dialysis treatment to go anywhere else. She should have been home hours ago.

I call her sister, crying. Mary hasn't heard from her either. I envision Charlene stretched across the kitchen linoleum, unable to get up. While Mary makes a few phone calls, I drive to Charlene's house, letting myself in with her hidden key—she's showed me, finally, where she keeps it.

I flip on the light to an empty kitchen and Nibaa wiggling and whimpering in her crate. I check the bedroom, the living room, and the bathroom, just in case. No Charlene.

Her telephone rings, and I pick up. It's Mary calling to say Charlene is in the emergency room in the Barron hospital. Her driver brought her the forty-five minutes home from dialysis, and, once home, Charlene called their brother Sam and asked him to take her the forty-five minutes back.

"I don't know why she didn't just stay up there," Mary grumbles.

"I hope she's okay."

"Oh, she has these bouts every winter—not that I'm not worried about her—but she's had them so often we're used to it."

"Really? What causes them?"

"She has COPD. You know, that dry little cough she does?" Mary demonstrates over the phone.

"What's COPD?"

Mary pauses, seemingly dumbfounded by my lack of knowledge. "Chronic obstructive pulmonary disease."

"Mary said you have COPD," I say to Charlene the next day, after I've hugged her and told her how glad I am that she's all right. "What's that?"

"It's another name for chronic bronchitis."

At home, I look it up online. Apparently, when you don't watch television, you miss a lot of things, such as the Smurfs and the names of pop stars and the number three killer of Americans. Pieces start to fall into place as I read about COPD online. So this is why Charlene's fingers are purple, why she coughs so much, and why she hasn't been able to get her breath in dialysis. She's killing herself by smoking, and she won't admit it.

She lied. I feel my anger rise.

"You lied to me," I say the next time I see her. I sit on the rocking chair, Charlene on the recliner, with Nibaa cavorting between us, shaking a red rag that used to be a stuffed horse. "COPD comes from smoking, and it's the third leading cause of death in America."

"I didn't lie to you!"

"Yes, you did. COPD includes emphysema, when your air sacs are weakened, and chronic bronchitis, when your lungs are infected. It means your lungs are permanently damaged."

"You sure know a lot about it all of a sudden."

"It's stupid to keep on smoking when you're killing yourself."

She straightens. "People have been telling me to stop smoking all my life. I smoke because I want to."

"You smoke because you can't stop."

She pauses. "Maybe."

"I don't know how you can claim to be a Christian when you smoke and lie and are angry and unforgiving."

Charlene, who has remained stone-faced and hard, puts her head back against the recliner. "Don't," she says, her voice quiet.

I've hurt her. This satisfies me.

She walks out to the kitchen table, and I follow. She picks up her playing cards, shuffles them, and starts a game of solitaire, snapping the cards neatly into their places, row on row, while I watch.

"You need to let God change your heart so you can have victory over your anger and over your smoking."

Charlene slaps her cards onto the table, grabs a cigarette, lights it, and takes a long, deliberate puff. "My smoking bugs the spit out of you, doesn't it?"

She is right, and the realization makes me smile. "Yeah."

Charlene's face calms, dropping from anger into acceptance and weariness.

When I put on my coat and boots later, I wait for my goodbye hug, just like I always do, and Charlene stands up to give it to me, just like she always does.

"I'm sorry I lied to you. I didn't mean to."

I don't believe you, I tell her with my eyes.

"I didn't think of it that way."

I believe her, and my anger leaves.

I bring Charlene two blue jay feathers the next day, small and delicate, striped in black. "Blue for the sky," I tell her, "and blue for forgetfulness, because God says his mercy toward us is as great as the heavens are from the earth, and he'll remove our sins as far as the east is from the west."

I want her to know, despite all her wrongs, there is forgiveness with God.

She smiles with one side of her mouth. "Mary called today and gave it to me about my smoking too. So with my two best friends down on me, I'm feeling pretty low."

The next day, I travel to Indiana with my family for my paternal grandpa's funeral. He held on for days following a stroke, but we've expected this death. I call Charlene from my grandma's basement, perched on a floor mattress where someone will sleep.

"This is a surprise," she says, her voice warm. "I didn't expect to hear from you at all while you were gone."

"Yeah, I wanted to call and let you know we got here safe and see how you were doing."

"Well, I proved to myself I can quit smoking. I had only five cigarettes yesterday."

"Wow, Charlene, good for you!"

I am exuberant.

People pack the benches at Grandpa Miller's funeral. After the sermon, I stand up front with the other grandchildren to sing a song about heaven. Aunt Grace lifts her hands.

Then each of Grandpa's five children stand on the stage and talk about their heritage of faith. They remember his prayers and how he had a notebook written full of the names of people he prayed for. He prayed for each of his twenty-two grandchildren by name every day.

Dad, standing on stage beside his siblings, looks small and thin in comparison to the others, his broad forehead shining in the overhead lights, his tanned farmer skin dark in contrast to his long-sleeved, white dress shirt.

He smiles while he talks, at ease on the stage, adding a lighthearted touch to the others' heavier remembrances. "I remember my dad used to say 'There's so much good in the worst of us, and so much bad in the best of us, it hardly behooves any of us to talk about the rest of us.'"

The quote reminds me of Charlene. I picture her, alone in her small house, and wonder how she's doing. "No one will come to my funeral when I die," she told me once. My conscience smites me, belatedly, for telling her off.

Back in Wisconsin, after the funeral, I bring up the subject. "Thank you for forgiving me for the way I acted that time."

Charlene nods, smiling from her eyes. "It's easy to forgive you. I love you so much."

Charlene stands in the middle of the kitchen, arms open to greet me. We hug, but afterward she doesn't pull away. Gently, she runs her fingers down both sides of my face. Lightly, hands cradling my chin, she pecks me on the lips.

I do not back away.

I remember how, when I took her with me to church a few weeks ago, she claimed to see my grandpa take a man's face in his hands and kiss him on the lips. She's wrong, of course. Although my church does practice the holy kiss, woman to woman or man to man, we always shake hands and give a quick cheek kiss. It's true the older people often kiss on the lips, but I've never seen my grandpa take someone's face in his hands in the intimate way she described.

I hate how she must have thought her kiss through and planned it as a special welcome, wanting it, believing if she stays within my "culture," I won't think it wrong.

Back out in the car, all I want to do is scrub at my lips until the kiss is gone.

"You know that TV advertisement where an elephant stands on the person's chest, making it hard to breathe?" Charlene asks.

I shake my head. "No, I haven't seen that one."

"Oh. Well, that's exactly what it feels like."

Charlene's cough hasn't gotten any better. She puts her head down to cough—a dry cough with no substance to it—and unable to catch her breath, has to keep coughing and coughing.

She's terrified to be alone when she has a bad spell, terrified she will choke to death alone. She calls me one day. "Luci, could you come? I'm not doing well."

I call my sister to tell her I won't be able to make our shopping trip and go.

Charlene sits in her recliner, coughing and miserable. I sit across from her, wondering how to help.

Mary calls to talk to me. "She needs to go to the emergency room. I don't think she should be left alone. Would you take her, Luci? Tell her I said she should go."

"Here, I'll let you talk to her." I hand the phone to Charlene.

And Charlene, whom I would never dare to boss, is meek and pliable in her sister's hands. But she remains reluctant.

"The emergency room won't help me," she says, after she hangs up the phone. "They're just a band-aid clinic here in Rusk County."

"I think you'd better go. I'll start the car."

Thankfully, she doesn't argue. At the hospital, I walk her in through the emergency room doors and go to park my car. I find her afterward, refusing to give straight answers to the receptionist's questions, her face twisted with impatience. The receptionist's face looks strained. I smooth a conciliatory smile onto my face, along with what's meant to be a distant look, informing everyone I am only the driver and not responsible for any unpleasantness.

A nurse shows us into a bare tiled room equipped with a bed, a curtain divider, and two pink visitors' chairs. She helps Charlene to the edge of the bed, and Charlene sits with her arms propped stiffly on either side of her, her blue-jeaned legs dangling like a little girl's.

I sit in one of the visitors' chairs, studying her face in this unfamiliar environment—the wide slash of a mouth, the familiar labyrinth of wrinkles, every wrinkle now downturned and tense. Her lips are purple, the skin around them tinged with blue, her fingers thin, wrists brittle against the bed.

Two young aides enter with a hospital gown. One of them leans over Charlene and reaches to unbutton her shirt. "Can I help you put on this gown?"

Charlene swears at her, yelling that she should get out.

The aide—she looks to be in her teens—drops the gown on the bed like guilty goods, and they both hurry from the room.

A nurse, a different one this time, with a flat nose and a mannish haircut, comes with a clipboard and more questions. Her demeanor is professional but brusque as she asks for Charlene's name, address, and date of birth—the same information Charlene gave the receptionist earlier.

"Do you have COPD, Charlene?"

Charlene remains silent.

"Do you have COPD?" the nurse prods again.

At last, Charlene speaks. "Well, one doctor called it COPD, and the other doctor said I had chronic bronchitis."

"Which is pretty much the same thing, isn't it." The nurse puts it as a statement, not a question. "How many cigarettes do you smoke a day?"

A long pause. "Yesterday, I had three."

"How many would it be on a good day?"

"On a good day ... ten."

"I'll just put down six to ten, then." The nurse snaps her pen onto the clipboard. "Is there anything I can get you? A glass of water, maybe?"

"I don't want a glass of water. You can bring me a Jack Daniels."

The nurse laughs without amusement. "I'm sorry. We don't have Jack Daniels here."

"I have some out in the car."

Another nurse, this one young and pretty with bright blonde hair, pushes a wheelchair into the room. "I need to take you for a chest x-ray," she says, her voice loud and cheerful. She sets the brakes on the wheelchair. "Can I help you get in the chair?"

"No. I can stand just fine."

Charlene pushes herself slowly to her feet and stands for a moment, wobbling. I reach to help her, but the blonde nurse is quicker. She slips an arm through Charlene's until she regains her balance and then lowers her gently to the wheelchair. As soon as Charlene sits down, she begins coughing in that way she has when she can't catch her breath. When the coughing stops, finally, the nurse wheels her away.

They're back fifteen minutes later and the blonde nurse helps Charlene from the wheelchair to the edge of the bed. "Your hands are so cold. Would you like a warm blanket?"

"No."

"Is there anything else I can do for you?"

"Yes, you can give me a shot and put me to sleep."

The nurse smiles brightly and leans closer, a mixture of sympathy and annoyance. "I'm sorry, that's the one thing I can't do for you."

She leaves and we are alone again, eyeing each other across the white tiled floor—Charlene perched stiffly on the edge of the bed, me leaning back in the pale pink visitors' chair, my hands in the pockets of my jacket.

The muscles in her face have relaxed now that the nurses are gone. "I love you," she says suddenly.

"I love you, too."

"It's embarrassing for me—to have you see me as a crotchety old lady."

"I always knew you were a crotchety old lady, anyway."

"Oh." Her straight eyebrows raise a fraction.

"Just teasing," I say quickly. "You're not crotchety." I look at her dangling legs. "Are you comfortable there? You could come over and sit on this other chair beside me."

She considers. "All right." She slides carefully forward until her feet touch the floor, then steps slowly to the chair and sits down, her back straight and well away from the back rest. "How long are they going to make us wait? Hurry up and wait. That's the story of my life."

Her hands against her blue jeans are slender, fragile, and faintly purple. I feel a sudden urge to pick one of the hands up and hold it, to sit with her small hand resting in mine. But that would be weird. Lesbian.

"Your hands look cold," I say. "Are you cold?" I pick up her hand and study it, feel its slim coolness.

She sits very still, looking straight ahead. Her hand remains limp, but her chest heaves violently, and her breath comes fast.

I feel like a god suddenly, with a power I didn't know I had. The power to wrap a life around my little finger or crush it in my palm.

Mary arrives just in time to see Charlene refuse the EKG the doctor ordered. "I don't need that! I'll be fine as soon as I get home."

Mary's eyes are dark and tired, her face impatient. "Do you want to step out for a cup of coffee?" she asks me. She leads the way to the lounge, her boots clicking on tiles. We drink our coffee standing by the coffee dispenser, sipping from white Styrofoam cups. "Char makes me so mad," she says. "Why does she act like this? Do you notice how she acts so sick at home, and then as soon as she gets here she's fine?"

"She hates hospitals," I say. "She's had so many surgeries. And she was with your mom when she died in the hospital."

Charlene had been with her mother after a mundane surgery, the other siblings and their dad all gone to get something to eat. "Could I have a drink?" her mother asked, and Charlene went to find her one. When she stepped into the room a few minutes later, a glass of water in her hand, her mother's face had changed, and Charlene heard the strange stillness of the end of breath. The room grew ice cold at that moment, just as cold as if she were standing outside in snow. The glass dropped from her hand and shattered on the floor.

"I knew then I'd experienced something," Charlene told me. "I didn't know what it was then, but now I realize it was Jesus coming into the room to take her to heaven."

I've heard of the coldness of ghosts, but never the coldness of Jesus. I didn't argue, though. It wasn't my mother who died.

Now, I look at Mary's impatient face and wonder how to bridge the gap between sisters. "I think she's scared she'll die in the hospital."

"I don't think she should be at home alone," Mary says. "Not when she's sick like this. I wonder how she would feel about going to a nursing home."

"She would hate it."

When we return to Charlene's room, her face looks flushed, and I know she is feeling betrayed, wondering what we've been saying about her.

"I have to get to work," I tell her, giving her a hug. "I love you. I'll call later to see how you're doing."

Her wrinkles relax, just a fraction.

I am relieved when Charlene returns home later that day, but I wonder at Charlene's family relationships.

When they were young, her brothers scrapped like tigers. "My mom would get the car ready when she saw John and Emmet fighting," Charlene told me once, "because she knew that, sooner or later, someone would get hurt. Then off they would go to the doctor."

I could hardly believe a parent would be so lax. "Maybe that's why your family turned out every which way."

"Maybe."

She tells me about her brother John. Five years older than Charlene, he made her life miserable with teasing. One day, when she was still small, he grabbed her doll away from her, yanked off the head, and tossed it to another brother.

"Here, catch!"

Charlene ran to her mother, crying.

"Why would you do such a thing?" her mother asked him.

"If the head is on the doll, only she can play with it," he said. "If we use it for a ball, we can all have fun with it."

When Charlene was older, she worked a whole year to earn the money to buy herself a bike. When she turned twelve, she finally had enough to go into town and buy a shiny red bike. When she rode it, she felt she was flying.

On a day during harvest, she biked down the road to get the mail where the Brands and several neighboring farmers had their mailboxes. She found a car track that rode smooth and she pedaled for all she was worth—bike chain whirring under blue-jeaned legs, spokes purring, tires jouncing over ruts. When she got back to the house, hot and panting, it was time for lunch, and Grandma came out to call the men. Charlene laid her bike down in the grass.

During a strenuous harvest, horses also must break and eat. Emmet and John were told to water them, and John, showing off, rode his horse in a wide circle around the yard to the water trough. He "accidentally" walked the horse right over Charlene's new bike, lying in the grass.

Screaming at him, she ran to her bike to examine the damage. Both tires were dented, the spokes broken and splayed in odd directions. The bike would never fly again.

With all her soul, Charlene knew that he hated her.

John lived out West now, and Charlene only saw him at family reunions.

"I love him, but I just don't like him," she says every time she mentions him to me.

This is the loyalty of her, claiming love where she cannot choose like. She loves all her brothers and sisters passionately but can't get along with any of them. Even her relationship with Mary, the special sister ten years younger than herself, seems rocky. They are constantly having spats. Once, in the heat of anger, Charlene slams down the phone on Mary and then is petrified Mary won't forgive her.

"Oh, that's okay. I understand how old people are," Mary says when Charlene apologizes.

"That's the first time she's ever called me old," Charlene tells me. She doesn't seem offended, only relieved.

"Mary can't ever sit down and talk to me face to face," she says another time. "She'll talk a mile a minute to anyone else who visits, but whenever I'm at her house and sit down across from her, she'll get up and go somewhere else. I don't understand why. She'll talk to me for hours over the phone."

Once when the weather is warm and the roads good, she makes plans to drive over to Mary's place to pick up her tackle box.

"I'll be gone, and Ron will be sleeping," Mary says. "But the garage door will be open, and the tackle box is in the garage."

"If you're going to be gone, I'll pick it up another day," Charlene says.

"You can come get it while I'm gone!" Mary says, annoyed by such senselessness. "It's just sitting out in the garage."

"No, I'll wait and come another time."

"Suit yourself."

"You probably want to go when she's home because you'd like the chance to see her," I say when Charlene tells me about the conversation.

She looks taken aback. Maybe she thought no one else comprehended her minor manipulations. I sometimes suspect that the small jobs and errands she hatches now and then for Mary to do are hatched mainly from a desire to see her.

"You should tell Mary you miss her and want to see her," I say. "She'd understand that. She's your sister."

Charlene looks away from me, out the window toward the bird feeder. "The ladderback was at the feeder again this morning. We'll have to get some more suet."

Charlene shows me a shiny black jacket—never before worn—hanging in her guest room closet. The name of her favorite music artist—"Liberace"—is emblazoned across its back. "I'll tell you about Liberace sometime," she says. By the significance in her voice, I know this must be important.

About a week later, I sit at the kitchen table, chopping carrots for chicken soup. I've already spent the morning in town with Charlene, driving her over the snowy-cold streets, offering an arm to walk her into the grocery store, and sitting with her at American Family Insurance while she has her policy reviewed. I meant to only spend a couple of hours with Charlene, not the largest part of my day. I feel, as I do so often, that she takes me for granted, liberally wasting minutes that are not hers.

And now she wants to make chicken soup.

She's cooked the chicken this morning and told me about it on the way back from town. When I lifted the lid and saw the heavy cooked chicken inside, slimy with grease, I couldn't imagine her with her slow movements and frail body lifting it out, picking the meat off, chopping the vegetables.

"Sure," I say. "I can stay and help."

So now I sit at the table and chop carrots, still wearing the puffy white coat I wore into town, impatient to be done and gone. "You wanted to tell me about Liberace sometime, Char," I say to pass the time.

"He was the greatest pianist that ever lived," Charlene says, speaking in that deliberate way she has, "but he was gay, so then he wasn't great anymore." She moves slowly across the kitchen, a paring knife in her hand, and sits down across from me.

Suddenly, I'm not thinking about going home anymore. This pot of chicken soup has become vitally interesting, and the one thing I've never dared ask about has become fair game.

"What do you think about gay?" she asks.

"Well," I say, carefully choosing my words, "I think it's a sin in God's eyes. But I don't think it's any worse than lying or stealing or getting divorced. In God's eyes, we are all sinners."

In theory, I believe this. In reality, the thought of same sex grosses me out.

"There is only one place in the New Testament that mentions it," I tell her. I pick up her Bible and read her the verses from Romans: "... for even their women did change the natural use into that which is against nature ... receiving in themselves that recompense of their error which was meet." I look at her intent face. "Do you want me to write down the reference for you?"

She nods.

"Then God talks about it in the Old Testament law. I didn't even know these verses were here until just recently." Because I looked for them. I had no reason to be interested before I met Charlene. I read her the two separate passages from Leviticus. "'Thou shalt not lie with mankind, as with womankind: it is abomination,' and 'If a man also lie with mankind, as he lieth with a woman, both of them have committed an abomination: they shall surely be put to death; their blood shall be upon them.'" My voice trembles as I read. The verses come right next to passages that forbid a man to lie with a beast or to uncover the nakedness of his sister.

Charlene listens quietly. This is not news to her, I realize. The bookmark in her Bible is past Leviticus, in Deuteronomy, and she would have taken note. Of course.

"I was bisexual when I was young." Her voice sounds callous now, rough. "Man or woman, I didn't care. I slept with them all."

I nod and continue to chop carrots. Charlene gets up and walks around the table, pretends to do something with the phone on the stand beside me. Then she lays her hand on my coat sleeve, the pressure faint against the puffiness. "I don't care if it's wrong. I love you anyway."

She thinks she's losing me, I realize, and my heart aches for her. She thinks after this, I'll be gone.

I smile enthusiastically, pretending not to catch the portent of her words. "I love you too."

I am glad to finally know. I have been second-guessing myself. *Maybe that didn't mean anything, maybe that's normal for her, maybe I imagined things.* But now she's told me, and I know I'm not crazy, not imagining things, not reading a universe of thought into dots of happenstance.

I remember the dark regret in her eyes when she said, "I did things when I was young I would never do now." She doesn't talk often of the dark part of her past. When she does, I pay attention.

Charlene's first job out of high school was at a Laundromat in Ladysmith. She borrowed enough money from her dad to buy her first car, then worked like a horse all summer to pay him back.

She was like her dad in many ways: hard-working, impatient, and easily angered. They drank hard and swore hard. He took her fishing. She was the only one of the children who got along with him because they were drinking buddies.

When Charlene heard about a high-paying factory job in Rockford, Illinois, she moved there. She worked through the week and drank on the weekends. One day, she woke up with such a hangover she thought her head would burst. She walked down the street toward the nearest bar to buy herself a drink, and her head hurt so bad, it knocked her down in the street.

She lay there, unconscious of anything but her brain ramming against her skull. After a long time, she got up and staggered home.

"I decided if that's the way the Creator feels about it, I'm never drinking again," she told me about that experience.

And as long as I've known her, she never has, except for cans of "pretend beer" she keeps in her refrigerator.

"I was never really attracted to men," Charlene tells me. "They were rough and tough and crude."

I nod, thinking I understand. Charlene grew up with men, worked like a man, cussed like a man. She admires gentleness.

But then she pauses and looks at me. "We were just born with masculine tendencies."

Is she including me with herself? I remember telling her I never found a guy good enough. Maybe she misunderstood. "I'm not masculine."

A picture rises in my mind: Charlene's love of beauty; her precise, ordered days; her large curiosity; her small manipulations; her emotions; her vanities; and inept as her body is, the defined grace of her movements. Men are a mystery, but I know women.

"And you seem like a feminine person to me."

She smiles, pleased. Probably she's not accustomed to being called feminine.

"Well, I like to think so," she says.

JANUARY 2012

I ask, "Do you want to go to the Ladysmith Family Restaurant or to the Back Door Café?" as I back out of the driveway onto the snow-slushed street. I know Charlene likes the Back Door Café best, but we've eaten there so often I am sick of it.

"I don't care!" she says, her tone of voice adding, *You idiot*.

Frantically, I deliberate. Making decisions is not my strong point, but I don't want to look weak in front of Char the All-Knowing.

"We'll go to the Back Door, I guess."

We're already headed in that direction, and she probably wants to go there anyway. Unlike me, Charlene has no dislike for ritual or sameness.

As I pull the car up to the café, I wish I had chosen differently. The Back Door sits in the middle of a strip of buildings along a sidewalk, and on this blustery day, ice and snow are packed a foot from the curb. I see a parking place open directly in front of the restaurant, but I'll have to parallel park, something I haven't done more than once or twice since drivers' ed.

I pull up beside the vehicle in front of the space and back toward the other, swinging the car's rear bumper in and turning the wheel sharp. My effort lands us three feet out from the curb. I pull forward and back again, this time my front bumper inching so perilously close to the first vehicle I have to stop. Forward and back. Forward and back.

Charlene, tense on the seat beside me, barks instructions. If there is anything at all going on in the world, Charlene knows exactly what to do and how to go about doing it, and she's never stingy with her knowledge.

I hate the bossy insistence of her voice, hate the way it drones around my head like a fat summer fly, and hate the way my mind tangles and tenses in response. I try to tune out her instructions and concentrate on parking.

After the fourth attempt, Charlene flings open the car door and leaps onto the sidewalk through the snow, spouting curses over her shoulder at me. She flounces into the restaurant. I have never seen her so agile.

I park the car, finding it much easier to do so without her sitting beside me, and walk calmly into the restaurant. Charlene sits alone at a table, drinking a chocolate Pepsi, and I smile and sit down across from her as if nothing happened. I pity her because she can't control her impatience or her temper—the result of years of loneliness and unhappiness—and won't give any retribution but love.

One evening a few days later, my mom and sisters drop me off at Charlene's on their way into town. "Come in!" she calls from the living room when I call "knock-knock" at the door. I stop to pet Nibaa, who is bouncing, overjoyed, against my legs, then go into the living room and sit in the rocker across from Charlene's recliner. I am in a good mood, chattering and happy, burbling whatever thought pops into my mind.

"It's kinda strange, Char, to think about how people always see themselves differently than other people see them. It's hard to know how other people see you because you can only see yourself."

I have often wondered how other people see me. Do they think I'm honest or wishy-washy, shy or direct, intelligent or half-brained?

"How do you think of me, Char?"

I would not normally ask anyone such a question for fear of shattering my fragile ego. But in the near darkness of the mellow lamplight, sitting with Charlene who loves me, I feel safe. And Charlene is always honest. She won't give a nice answer just to please me.

She straightens in her chair as though she has been waiting for this question.

"I think you want to change me," she says, her voice harsh. "All my life, people have tried to change me. And I don't want to be changed."

I can feel my face heat, the red rising to my neck and ears.

She continues, pausing to consider her words now. "I don't know ... I've never experienced anyone like you before. You analyze everything I say, and you don't really listen to what I'm saying. People say things they don't mean, Luci. They make jokes. The Indians believed it was important to laugh. You need to laugh more. You have no sense of humor."

The motions of the room slow, and I am outside it—outside the moment and eternally within it—my senses stiff and withdrawn.

I am a child again, weeping in my room because I have overheard one of my sisters making an unkind comment about me. I know from this that they all hate me and talk about me behind my back.

I am a teenager, sweet and oversensitive and self-conscious, walking the halls at a three-week winter Bible school populated by young people. The students are a mix of fun, friendly, and confident and awkward, bulky, and odd. And I, afraid of the cool group and ashamed of the others, connect only fleetingly with a few. No one hates me and no one loves me because no one really knows me. I constantly wear a smile on my face because I want everyone to think I am enjoying myself, that I have friends somewhere, just around a corner.

I am a young adult, more confident, but still commonly described as "sweet"—a word I both love and hate. Hate, because it defines me as passive and without spine. Love, because it protects me. People treat me kindly because I am sweet. No one has ever, until this moment, in this room, dissed me to my face.

"I told Mary how we were parking in front of the Back Door Café the other day," Charlene says, "and how you wouldn't listen to me, and I jumped out and swore at you. She wondered what you said, and I said, 'Not much.' Now with Mary, it's different. When she took me to town the other day, as I climbed into the truck I knocked her jar of change all over the seat and the grocery store parking lot. She said, 'You clumsy jerk, now pick it up!' And then she looked around and said, 'I hope nobody heard that.'

"Mary and I always say what we think to each other, and then it's over and done with. It might take her a little longer than me to get over it, but she comes around after a few days. With you, I never know what you're thinking."

I sit stiff in my chair. "So you'd like me to say what I think more?"

She nods.

As I drive home, I repeat over and over the injustice of how I spend time with Charlene, do for her whatever she wants done with no pay, put up with her anger, her moods, and her sharp tongue ... and this is what she has to say to me? That I don't listen? Listening is the one thing I thought I was good at. And does she really want another relationship like the one she has with her sister? Every time I talk to Mary, she seems upset with Charlene, and Charlene is always complaining about Mary.

But the thing that rankles me most is that she said I have no sense of humor. If there's one thing I thought I would never be accused of, it's that. I am proud of my sense of humor. It's my insulation from a harsh world.

So she wants me to be honest? What does she want me to say? Since my early attempts to help her become born again and my one harsh sweep of her character, I have avoided words, leaning instead on smiles and gentle kindness. With Charlene, I've discovered a truth I never learned in hundreds of sermons and self-help articles that tend to preach the opposite.

The truth is this: Words separate. Silence bridges.

Between minds lie distances greater than Siberia. Don't ever tell people what you think. As long as you remain silent, they will assume you think as they do, and friendship is possible.

Still, Charlene asked for the words. She claims she wants me to tell her what I think.

What do I think? I try to slow my heated mind.

I know I want to preserve this friendship. I also know some people seem to thrive on honesty and passion and strained relationships, but I cannot. I can't build a friendship based on hurt. Besides, whatever Charlene says, her skin is about as thick as a newborn babe's. Mine is figgy by comparison.

She might handle criticism better outwardly, but the hurt remains in her longer. Her emotional center is weak, the air sacs worn with hurts from the past, the pink-black tissue floppy and sagging.

And she is alone.

When I hurt, I cry for three days and then tell Mom about it. After that I am okay.

When Charlene hurts, she does not cry. She only remembers, and that is worse.

As I near home, my mind calms. I can see blue through the trees, and reach for it, excited. Out of the multitude of truths I could give Charlene, one emerges like a crystal snowflake. I only need her to know one thing and now, freed from the cloying sweetness of her gratitude, I can tell her.

Love constricts. Criticism gives wings.

I call her the next morning. "I thought of what I wanted to tell you. Can I come over and talk to you?"

"Sure, come over."

I know she will be on pins and needles, wondering, waiting to be hurt, and I am glad.

Her house is nice this early time of day. Quiet, because she hasn't yet turned on the television, and the air feels cleaner, less smoky than it does in the afternoons. I sit down across the table from her.

She waits.

I take a deep breath. I've already formulated the words in my mind.

"I don't want to change you. I like you just the way you are. And I can't help how I am either. If you get tired of me analyzing everything you say, just think how it would feel to be me and live with that. I analyze everything in my mind, and I go in circles and circles and circles, thinking about things, and I can't stop. I get tired of it. And it's not true that I don't have a sense of humor. I do. You just haven't got to know that side of me yet."

Charlene is all smile and warm relief. "And that is what I'm hoping for."

I smile back at her, reach for my one truth, and set it on the table, gentle, so she won't think it a punishment. "I'd like to maybe not come over quite so often, so I have more time to write and do things at home. I'd like to have a little more space, maybe take more days off from seeing you and not call you every day I don't work."

She digests that. "So I should just add you to my list of people to call if I need help."

"Yes," I say, relieved.

She pushes back her chair. "Well, I need to make oatmeal cookies today, so if you don't mind, I'll get started."

Charlene always takes one or two oatmeal cookies along on every dialysis trip as a necessary energizer, and I always help her make them. The stiff cookie dough is too much for her frail arm and wrist muscles to handle.

"I can mix the dough for you before I go," I say. I pull the red plastic mixing bowl from the cupboard and take a stick of butter from the refrigerator. I cut the butter in half, put the two halves into a coffee cup, and put the coffee cup into the microwave, just the way she showed me she likes it done.

I'm careful to cover the top of the coffee cup with a paper towel. The first time I melted butter in her microwave, I didn't use a paper towel, and the butter popped and splattered. "Well, now the microwave's been christened," she said.

I put the melted butter into the mixing bowl with the oatmeal, the brown sugar, the flour, cinnamon, baking soda, raisins. Charlene sits at the table, watching. I am grateful I had a chance to ask for my space and grateful to her for accepting what I thought would be a difficult request.

"I really respect you for not smoking so much," I tell her, wanting to build her up, "and for telling me you used to be bisexual. I wanted to ask, but I didn't, because I was afraid you would lie to me."

"I told you I was bisexual because that was easier than telling you I was homosexual for fifteen years."

"You were?"

She nods. "I never told anyone in my family. They might have guessed, but I didn't tell them."

But she told me. I feel honored. I take the bowl of cookie ingredients and the big spoon and sit down on the chair across from her to finish mixing.

"I don't understand why it would be wrong," Charlene says, "when people who are gay can't help the way they are."

She's voiced exactly what I've thought through again and again. Yet, my verdict has never seemed quite as true as now, when I am trying to make Charlene understand.

"We are all born in sin," I say. "Some people have a tendency toward one thing, and some a tendency toward another, but we all have weaknesses and sins. Just because people can't help something doesn't make it right."

I scrape the bottom of the bowl with my spoon, scooping plain dough up toward a cluster of raisins.

"When my dad was young, before he became a Christian, he was ... what's that word ... a compulsive stealer. Whenever he went to somebody's house, he would take something. It didn't matter what he took, as long as he took something. If he would have stolen a car one day and gone to court for it, no jury in the land would have told him, 'Well, you can't help that you want to steal things, so it's okay.'"

Charlene smiles, approbation in her eyes. "Thank you for explaining these things to me, Luci."

I hear real gratitude in her voice.

To me, it's the strangest sensation ever, to explain to someone their sin and to know that they are grateful.

PART THREE—THINGS DESIRED

I did not know what to do with it.
I had never had a heart.

After telling Charlene I want more space, I do pretty well with taking time off. For a couple of weeks anyway.

If only I wasn't cursed with a weak will, a demanding heart, and a conscience self-diagnosed with OCD. Every day I don't visit, I feel guilty. I spend hours worrying about her, wondering if she is lonely or depressed, if the day stretches long ahead of her, and if she is missing me.

I picture her vividly—playing solitaire, smoking, letting Nibaa out, watching television, watching the clock all the long day for the fifteen minutes I will visit over my supper break.

I imagine her planning her simple meals—broccoli maybe, and noodles with butter but no salt, due to dialysis restrictions. She will start planning hours ahead so when the time comes she will have worked up an appetite. Charlene is down to ninety-six pounds in her jeans and tennis shoes now. She seldom feels hungry and has to force herself to eat.

I know she lives for my visits.

And because she lives for me, I am bound to this life, this town, this job. I would like more time to write, to travel, to go on the mission field, but I can no longer enjoy even a short trip with Charlene at home waiting.

Part of me hates her and feels used by her. Her need is a strong talon holding me suspended above the ground. A path lies below—possibility, a future—mysterious and haunting and winding between trees, but I cannot follow it.

I hang, panting.

About a week after I tell Charlene I want more space, she says, "I've been thinking. You don't have to come see me so much. If you come help me once a week, on Mondays, that's all you have to come." She pauses, and her next words are quieter, drifting into cracks. "And if you don't want to come then, you don't have to."

Why is it that I long for freedom and when it's offered, don't take it?

Something about the hesitant voice, the hooded eyes.

The next time I vacuum for her, she holds out a twenty-dollar bill.

"What's that for?"

"You used a lot of energy today, vacuuming for me."

"Keep your money. I don't want it," I say violently.

She puts it back into her pocket, satisfied.

Later, I sometimes regret my refusal. I watch Charlene receive large tribal-benefit checks in the mail, watch her give away chunks of money freely to other people, and resent it. So she's not as poor as she's made herself out to be. I wonder if she cares about me at all, or if she only takes advantage of me.

Funny thing is, if she were paying, I would never be willing to spend so many of my precious hours with her. I would measure time against money and refuse.

Money is a limiter. Money is cold.

Need is warm, asking.

And I can never say no.

I won't be taken advantage of, I decide, when I have grown desperate enough to make a decision. I need to have time for myself.

"I'm not coming to see you so often anymore," I tell Charlene the next time I visit. "Tomorrow's your dialysis day, so you won't be feeling good anyway, and then I have

Friday and the weekend off, so I won't be coming into town. I'll come see you in four days, on Monday. And I'll help you with whatever you need then."

Charlene's lined face remains flat and unsmiling, but she doesn't argue.

I worry about her the entire evening and the following morning until I can't stand it anymore. She is hurting. I know it. Four days is too long. The minute I think she'll be back from dialysis, I call.

"How are you?"

"Feeling a little wimpy." Her voice sounds ragged and raw, as if she has a bad cold.

Did I do this to her simply by saying I won't visit?

"I'll come by on my way to work."

When I arrive, Charlene sits in her recliner. She's set slippers out for me on the footstool in front of the rocking chair. "So your footsies won't get cold," she says, smiling.

I put the slippers on, kneel beside her chair, and take her cool purple hand. "How are you doing?"

She looks as if she's been through a violent illness.

"I thought you weren't coming to see me."

"I couldn't bear not to."

A few days later, I make another attempt, this time more gently. "Is it okay if I don't come to see you every day?"

"No!" The words are bottled and quick. "If I can just see you a little bit every day. A couple minutes is all I need."

She pauses, thinks.

"I don't want you to think I'm crazy, that a couple minutes is as good as a couple hours. It does make a difference. But if I could compare it to breathing, maybe you will understand. A man who is holding his breath under water, if he takes a breath of air, then he can go back to holding his breath again." She shook her head. "But maybe you think I'm a crazy old woman."

"No," I say, and I can feel the softness in my face. "You're not crazy."

I try, valiantly. I drive uptown on my days off or ask someone from my family to drop me off when they're going to town. I clean her house, eat meals with her, and take her shopping. I stop in at her place before work or on my supper break, and sometimes both.

The hole in Charlene is enormous.

She lets me take her to my church sometimes and always comes to my house afterward for Sunday lunch. She thrives during these times—witty, sparky, smiling, absorbing the laughter and the friendship of my family.

"I don't know why I love your parents so much," she says once.

I've seen how she admires my parents, how she watches them and listens to them. "I think because they fill a need your parents never did. I mean, I know you love your parents, but they didn't give you what you needed to start in life."

Her eyes grow wide, fragile. I wonder if anyone has ever told her this before, and if she ever acknowledged it to herself. Charlene is always loyal, defending even her alcoholic father, but the gaps are wider than words can fill.

Finally, I crash. I hunch over the dining room table, crying to Dad, my frustration level at an all-time high. "I never have time to write, and when I do, my brain feels so fragmented I can't write anyway. I never see you guys because I'm always at work or at Char's. And all I want to do is write. I think I'm going to go down to part time at work."

Dad shakes his head. "If you have more free time, Charlene will just use that up. You need to have a reason to be away from her."

"If I had more free time, I could use it to write."

"It won't work out that way. Charlene would know you had those days off, and she would think of reasons for you to be over there. If you want more time to write, take time off from Charlene, not from your job."

"I try to take time off from Charlene, but I don't know how. She needs me and misses me so much." I lean over the table, crying, my body shuddering with the effort to keep the sobs inside.

"Listen to me, Luci. Charlene isn't really your friend. All she's doing is manipulating you because she knows she can."

I wonder if he is right. He hasn't seen her, needy and trembling, as I have. But he sounds so sure. "Why would she do that?"

He shrugs. "Sometimes older people have had disappointments in life, and that's the only thing they have left. You need to have some freedom from her. You need to have time to do the things Luci wants to do. I miss the old happy Luci and I want the old happy Luci back. Now I'm going to tell you something, and I want you to listen to me."

His voice is stern. Dad hasn't told me what to do, not even to make suggestions, in a very long time. The sensation is odd but comforting. My tears are mostly gone now. "What?"

"Will you listen to me?"

"Yes."

"You take your days off. You can go to see her on the days you work, but I want you to keep those two days a week you have off work completely free of Charlene."

I think of the two days—not just one day, but two—and how long they will seem to Charlene, stretching into eternity.

And how much like heaven to me.

There are old family pictures—me with my arms draped around a younger Dad's neck as he sits beside a campfire, another of me leaning up against him while he reads from a book. My hair is a very pale brown in these pictures and curled at the ends, my eyes like saucers, my nose like a button. Looking at them, I marvel at the young child's familiarity with her father. I cannot remember it.

What I remember is respect, mingled with fear.

I am a very little person in a world where everyone is bigger than me. I hate when people laugh at me or tease me, especially when it is Dad, with his smooth confident voice and laughing eyes.

After he hurts my feelings once, I go up to my room and compose a poem, the first I have ever written. The words are short and easy because I am still new to writing.

There once was a lad
Who had a dad
And he made him very,
Very, very sad.

I know the lad in the poem is really myself, and I am proud of this cleverness. No one reading the poem would know that unless I told them.

Writing the poem gives me great satisfaction, a feeling of revenge. Dad doesn't know, cannot know, that I am up here in my room writing a poem about him. He cannot know that in the quiet of my mind, I have exposed how mean he is and how he teases me.

I know my mom, who is sympathetic and gentle, loves me, but Dad ... I am afraid of him.

If you are too loud during his nap, he will come out of the bedroom, eyebrows furrowed, and give you a look that would melt metal. "That's enough now!" he will say.

Once he swats me for my noise, and I dribble a little bit in my red, white, and blue underwear with stars like an American flag. I am mortified, being six and far too old for such accidents. Quickly and secretly, I change them and put them down the laundry chute where no one will be the wiser.

I admire my dad from a distance. When he preaches Sunday mornings, I see how trim and handsome he is, more than any of the other dads in the church, and how his forehead beneath his dark hair shines, like he is holy. His voice rings with emotion. He tells stories, and sometimes he cries. I wince and look down at such times. I cannot look at him.

During my adolescent years, when I sit at the table eating dinner with my family, I resent every time Dad looks at me. I am sure he has seen me chewing with my mouth open and wonders how he birthed such a slop-pig daughter. I am sure he is noticing my fat stomach and the way it pooches the front of my dress.

I do not want to be noticed.

When I have achieved my late teens, I feel only relief to have made it through. Life is easier, less threatening, on this side of childhood.

At twenty-one, I move south to teach in a two-room Mennonite school. I have five students in three different grades and love every one of them. People view me differently here. At home, I was always the sweet, quiet one with a big smile. A bookworm. Here, I am the new girl and the schoolteacher. Parents invite me for dinner. The young people find me interesting and exciting. The children love me. I learn that confidence is a choice, and that fun and pretty and friendly are nothing more than an attitude.

I dare to think my own thoughts, dare at times to openly disagree with my dad. Disagreeing feels good, feels like throwing off shackles. Visiting home for the summer, I laugh at him once, laugh in his face, and he looks just as sheepish as anyone else who's being laughed at.

For the first time, I realize he is not invulnerable, not less prone to mistakes or hurt feelings than anyone else. He is only a man. The same man who told me stories about long-bearded dwarves when I was small. The man who used to take the whole family through the drive-thru at McDonald's and order thirteen hamburgers at a shot. The man who knelt beside me in the garden once, when I was crying, and told me in a voice as sure as oak and friendly as maple that I had a soft heart and that having a soft heart is a good thing.

He is only a man, but he is my dad.

He's made a point, since I've reached adulthood, of never telling me what to do.

Until now.

For the first time since I moved away to teach school, Dad is telling me with strong conviction exactly what to do. And it feels good. I feel that I have an advocate.

"I want to start keeping my days off to stay home," I tell Charlene the next time I see her.

"And I think you deserve those days off," she says, her voice full of warmth. "You work hard, and you deserve them. You need to have time to do what Luci wants to do."

"That's exactly what Dad said."

Her answer surprises me and fills me with gratitude. Charlene isn't only thinking of her own needs. She cares about mine too.

The days off are such freedom. Like Christmas.

Eventually, I start whittling them back. Because things happen on days off like doctor appointments and pharmacy pick-ups. And because it's hard for me to think of Charlene in her little house, alone.

But I try. I take more time for myself and tell Charlene beforehand what time I need to get home.

And Charlene tries. She is not so clingy and consciously gives me more space.

Every time I visit, Nibaa meets me at the door and jumps on me, wagging her tail, panting with gladness and energy.

"Don't jump all over Luci," Charlene scolds her one day. "You remind me of myself."

I am slipping my shoes off just inside the door and grin.

"Don't worry," Charlene says, petting Nibaa. "Luci loves you. But she might not if you don't leave her alone."

Whenever we say goodbye, we hug. Charlene's small body fits snugly into my arms, my chin just over her shoulder.

"I have my family, but my family doesn't matter," she says one day. "I live just to see you." She pulls back, looks at me. "Our friendship doesn't have to fit a label. It doesn't have to be a lesbian relationship."

I laugh to distance myself from her words. "I hope not. Otherwise I don't want to see you anymore."

She nods. "People have to label everything. Whether Mennonite or half-breed, they label you and that's what you are to them."

I understand. All my life, I've been labeled. Everywhere I go, people don't see a person. They see "Mennonite." Sometimes that's all they see.

"Labels aren't always so nice. But sometimes they give you a sense of security. You know who you are and where you belong."

"Yes," she says.

We understand each other in this, the Mennonite and the half-breed.

Early in our friendship, Charlene took offense at my church's practice of seating men and women separately during worship. She was every inch of her a feminist, and separated seating offended all her notions of equality. She argued with Grandpa at length on the subject—"So you think I'm not as good as you are?"—and came away believing she had trounced him soundly, while Grandpa, stout-faced and oblivious, didn't realize he'd been trounced.

"Separated seating doesn't have anything to do with the men being better than the women," I tried to explain. "It's just a practice, like shaking hands."

But Charlene, mind firmly embedded in her own culture, knew inequality when she saw it.

It was later, during an unrelated conversation, that she came to greater acceptance of what she considered senseless Mennonite practices.

Sitting at the Back Door Café one day, she complained to me about the injustice she endured growing up as a half-breed in a white society. She described how the other kids at school teased her and how she'd always been marked. "All my life I've been different."

"I know how you feel," I said. "I've always been different too. No matter where I go, I stand out, and people are always asking me questions about being a Mennonite. Maybe it doesn't feel quite the same, though, when you're different by choice and not by birth."

Realization dawned in her eyes.

Later, she slid the subject of Mennonite practices gently into a conversation, shame in her eyes. "I didn't understand."

Since that time, she's seldom been critical of the odd practices of my people. She doesn't ask, as others might, "Oh, don't you get hot in your long dress?" or "Aren't you cold without pants?" Or "Why can't you go to the fair?" She observes more than she asks, and when she asks, she asks to understand.

It's nice having a friend like that.

We finish a meal at the Back Door one day and are mincing our way toward the door, when a jolly, whiskery old farmer grins at me, motioning toward my head. "Is that a beekeeper's net you're wearing?"

I grin back.

"I've never heard it called that before, Luci," Charlene says.

"I haven't either." We go on out the door.

Back at the house, she says, "He really made me angry. I wanted to tell him off, but I didn't want to embarrass you."

"That's good you didn't, because it was none of your business."

Charlene looks pleased. She seldom gets me to say something spontaneous and angry.

"He was probably curious," I say. "But I wasn't going to satisfy his curiosity because he made me mad."

Her pleased look grows, a smile inside her face.

I think Charlene fears one possibility more than anything else.

The day she asked me to be her helpmeet, I told her, "I'm not tied to you. If I meet a guy and fall in love, I might move away with him."

I know she remembers that statement.

One day, as she sits across from me at the table, she makes a declaration, her voice firm and melodious. "I love you enough to be your person until you find the right person to love you. Until then, I will be there for you." Her dark eyes moisten. I do not want to think of Charlene as "my person," so I laugh and hurry to a different subject.

She speaks as though she is Nathan Hale, sacrificing her life for her soul's greatest loyalty.

I know she had many partners of her own, but she seldom talks about them to me. They are a part of the wild past Char, a woman I hold in a protected and curious spot in my mind, seeking to understand.

There is Whitey, a male. Charlene was engaged to him before she found out he was married with six children.

There was Trudy, whom she refers to as her roommate and hates. She took Trudy to see northern lights all a-dazzle above a parking lot, and Trudy was bored. Trudy was Catholic and a lying hypocrite. Whenever some old, treasured object of Charlene's turns up missing, she'll say, "Trudy must have taken it. She stole everything she could get her hands on."

There was Sue. She tells me about Sue one day at the Back Door Café. "We were together for fifteen years. When we broke up, I didn't want to live anymore."

Her eyes are dark pools, remembering.

"What was she like?" But I know instinctively. "Was she gentle?"

Charlene nods. "She could get along with anyone, got promoted to manager at the factory because everyone liked her."

"Why did you break up?"

"She used to get drunk every weekend. Didn't go to her own father's funeral, she was so drunk. And one day I thought, 'My mom lived with a weekend alcoholic all her life. And I'm not going to.' We stayed friends, and the next time she came around to the family reunion, she had herself"—Charlene's voice grows stretched and sarcastic—"a new little girlfriend. Well, when that girlfriend broke up with her because of her drinking, she decided to get help. Went to Alcoholics Anonymous and threw away all her alcohol."

Sue called and visited occasionally through the years. One day, Charlene pulls a pair of tennis shoes in a Walmart bag out of the closet. "I need to return these to Sue. She called today and said she's coming to visit sometime."

"Are you excited to see her?" I ask, feeling an odd twinge of jealousy.

Charlene looks at me blandly. "We're only friends, Luci."

The first time Charlene comes to church with me—after I invite her with pretended casualness and wait the days until Sunday, expecting her to change her mind—is an event. I pick her up at 9:40 Sunday morning and drive her out of town and over the bumpy ruts of Marshall Road to our church in the country. Charlene, dressed in tan slacks instead of her usual jeans, sits stiff in the passenger seat, her face tense.

Our church, a simple white-sided building with cement steps leading up to it, beckons from behind a gravel driveway. A row of pine trees edges the yard. I pull into the drive and look over at her tight face. "You don't have to be nervous. It's just us."

"I'm not nervous."

I pull up in front of the cement stairway and escort her to the door, wincing for her as she pulls herself up the banister one weary stair at a time. I had thought maybe one of my brothers could lift her inside, but Charlene will have nothing to do with the idea.

Vernon, with his drawled southern, "Hiaah," opens the door for us, grinning, crow's feet beside his eyes and bearded chin thrust forward. Char smiles back, and I think that when she smiles like this it is as if someone has taken all the spread-out joy of the world and concentrated it down into one tiny brown person.

We step into the brown-carpeted vestibule. Grandma rustles up to us, beaming, and takes one of Charlene's thin brown hands in both her plump ones. "I'm so happy you could come, Charlene!"

The church, with its yellowy-golden walls and stiff-napped brown carpet, seems different than I remember from other Sundays—browner, barer, less inviting. The people are friendly, though. I hadn't remembered just how friendly. They rally around Charlene with smiles and attention, and she expands into graciousness.

We move into the sanctuary, lined with clear glass windows, a wooden pulpit up front and wooden benches down both sides. Black-suited men sit on the right and ladies in dresses and head coverings on the left. I notice for the first time how stark we all look and how solemnly religious, like a batch of stiff Puritans.

Charlene pauses in the doorway. "Oh, that's right. I forgot the men and women have to sit separately."

"How could you forget?" I ask, laughing. I wish her voice wasn't so sharp and loud. Everyone seated in the auditorium can probably hear.

"What would they do to me if I went all the way down the aisle and sat beside your dad and Grandpa on the front bench?"

By the ministers? How awkward would that be?

But I shrug. "Nothing, I guess."

I wonder for a minute what I will do if she does. Will I sit beside her? That would be too embarrassing! Why can't she just conform and be sweet and gracious? People will think she is a crotchety old lady. Yet, somewhere along the way, she has become my old lady. I want to be proud of her.

Thankfully, Char doesn't follow through with her threat. We sit on the women's side, fifth bench from the back.

The song leader walks to the podium to lead the opening hymn. We all sing the words a cappella, Vernon's strong tenor voice blending with the bass and alto and soprano. "Break thou the bread of life, dear Lord to me." Beside me,

Charlene's back and her skinny body are straight and still, but her chest and belly heave, pushing her knitted sweater in and out.

She comes to church sometimes after that. I long for her to come, am joyful when she attends and sorrowful when she refuses. I never knew my church family was so important to me before I knew Charlene.

I talk to her often about spiritual things, partly to help her know the Lord and partly as a connector.

Despite the intensity of our relationship, a part of me feels alienated from her. Sequoia lengths lie between our minds, and Charlene, perhaps because of the pain she endures, is often snappish and impatient. Because she intimidates me, I never share more than a select few of my inner thoughts and feelings. I try most to hide my self-doubt because, in my mind, self-doubt is weakness. Charlene, who is strong, will be scornful.

But we both love God. Our love for him first drew us together and now keeps us connected.

In a moment of uneasy silence one day, trying to make conversation, I ask her a question on a spiritual subject.

She straightens in her chair. "All you talk about is God, God, God and Jesus, Jesus, Jesus, and I get sick and tired of it!"

Looking at the old woman sitting in the chair across from me, no civility or kindness in her face, I hate her and wonder why we are friends. If her need and fragility didn't pierce me, soak deep into me—if it weren't for that ... but I stop the thought there. If she weren't so needy, I still might love her. Charlene draws me.

As I drive home, I replay her words in my mind. I remember questions she's asked me about the Bible and how I answered them in my fast-paced, enthusiastic voice, my lips stuffed with knowledge, excited to tell what I knew. I listen hard to what she is saying: "I am sick and tired of your preaching. You are less than half my age, and not so wise as you think you are."

Despite her view of me, I am fairly skilled at listening.

"I like hearing from your dad and your grandpa," Charlene said to me pointedly, after a church service once. "They're old enough to have gained wisdom. We can learn from older people."

So I shut up about the Bible. Once, when she asks me a question about Scripture, I say, "I don't know." Her attitude seems to change after that. She is more open, less resentful. I marvel at the wisdom hidden in one tiny phrase.

I learned its power from my dad not long ago.

I am young. I ask questions.

Growing up conservative Mennonite in a world that lives and dresses far differently, there are many questions to ask.

Dad answers my questions, many of them more than once. He pulls explanations and simple logic straight from the Bible, and everything he says is honest and makes sense to me. He explains the Bible principles behind many of the distinctive Mennonite practices I question, but he never tries to pretend the Bible says something it does not.

I learn to think deep below the surface of things, to see into reasons, motives, and destinies.

Over the years, one question rises to the top of my mind and pushes the others away. I ask this question in many different forms to many different people. Always, I am angry. Never am I satisfied with the answers.

I ask Dad one day. Probably I have asked him before, but I do not remember his answer. "What about the people who never heard about Jesus?" I stand in front of the kitchen sink, facing him, sobbing. "Does God send them to hell when they never had a chance? How is that fair?"

I am angry, my heart in my hands.

"I don't know, Luci," he says.

I had thought he would come up with an explanation, and I had known the explanation wouldn't satisfy me.

But this ... there is tremendous release in these words: "I don't know." I begin to realize I don't need to know everything, and that not knowing is necessary to living.

I said the words first.

After a while, she said them back. After another while, she has stopped waiting for me. She screeches the words suddenly, joyfully, at odd moments—usually when I am concentrating, and love is the last thing on my mind.

"I love you, Luci," or "I love you, Luci Miller," and once, when we are both frustrated over the hanging of a shelf, "I love you anyway!"

I guard the words *I love you* more carefully than she does, feed them to her at what I consider the proper time and place, such as when we say goodbye. I keep my words quiet and a little dry, never passionate and surprising like Charlene's. That's because I worry about the rightness of our relationship.

We are so very close.

When two people come together day after day after day—one desperate for love and the other hungry to give it—when they work together through tiny necessities, when their habits and thought patterns become as familiar to each other as bread and cheese, the result is a relationship that is very like a marriage.

I worry that our friendship is somehow lesbian, and work to keep my love tightly controlled, knotted like the sinews beneath a tiger's skin. This only makes me feel I am passionate and trying to hide.

Sometimes I want to hold Charlene, to comfort her, to stroke her cheek and tell her, "Everything's gonna be all right, Char. It's okay." Then I worry those are lesbian emotions.

It's just that she is so small, a knotted ball that calls to all my nurturing instincts, a child who needs to sit in my lap and have the tears wiped away.

"I love you so much it's almost sinful," she says one day when I hug her goodbye. I know it is a confession, that this has been bothering her. "But I wouldn't let anything like that happen," she adds quickly. "Our friendship is too precious."

I do what I always do in these situations—ignore the obvious and pass on to something else. As though it is no big deal to me. Nothing I ever think about.

I accept her love, whatever mix of friendship and longing it might be, as part of the tremendous void that is her need. My own feelings are harder to gauge.

I worry I am really lesbian.

What does that mean, anyway? Does it have anything to do with how I sense Charlene's attraction for me ... and like it? With how I want her to think I am beautiful? Does it have anything to do with the way my body and my heart and my mind respond to her, reach for her, am satisfied by her?

Why don't I care much about guys anymore? Even Jake is mostly a memory.

"It's like I'm from a different planet than the girls at work," I tell her one day.

I've been talking about some of the aides I work with at the nursing home. Their world is a foreign one of boyfriends and apartment houses and making babies and sometimes partying, a world that makes me feel both young and old. Young, because they've had years of experience in sex, men, childbirth, debt—adult issues I've never dealt with.

Old, because they rush headlong into relationships and situations that make me cringe. They seem not to consider long-term consequences, and they never mention spiritual issues at all.

Nibaa, stretched out flat on her dog bed, sighs, sleeping and quiet for a change.

"All Fonda thinks about is getting a boyfriend. And some of those girls ... you should hear them talk. I just don't understand them. I mean, I don't even want to have sex. The thought of it scares me. I think I could like it, but it would have to be with the right person."

Charlene smiles, and her eyes are soft. "I know it would."

"I don't understand why these girls throw themselves away," I say. "I think sex is something to be treasured, like a rose. It's like if you try to rip open the bud too soon, you destroy the flower. You have to wait until the time is right, and then you have something beautiful."

Her eyes cup me gently, as though I am sacred, as though I am the rose to be treasured.

Saying goodbye, I hug her and ear touches cheek.

"Your ear is warm and mine is cold," she says, laughing.

I blush.

Warm weather hobbles in with much huffing and shuffling and changing of its mind. Spring is always so in Wisconsin. But one weekend, in a fit of inspiration, spring shakes out the remainder of old snow and sets green grass in its place.

The sun shines.

Charlene drives herself to dialysis.

I don't argue with her this time, nor offer to drive. When she arrives home safely after her first solo trip, I am proud. She has the look in her eye of someone who's accomplished great things.

"I decided if God can protect his special little Luci on the road, he can protect me too."

She still complains about Indianhead Transit Company and their unfair payment policies. One day, she asks me to take her to the old convent, where Indianhead offices are currently housed, to have it out with the CEO about a debt-collection letter she received.

Charlene stalks the woman to the depths of her private office, far at the end of the upstairs hallway. I trail her down the long hallway, peering into the little, white-walled rooms we pass—cells, they must be—and think about the nuns who slept there, praying the rosary beside their cots.

I once visited the nuns' cemetery on these very grounds and studied the flat slab tombstones rowed in the grass—all exactly the same, all facing east, past and personality shrouded by sameness. Every tombstone engraved with the name "Sister Mary." Sister Mary Theresa, Sister Mary Bernadine, Sister Mary Celinda, and so on. Mary must have been a popular name, I thought, until I saw that not just many, but all the tombstones carried this name. Later, I learned these were Servite sisters, dedicated and named for the service of Mary.

At the end of the long hallway, we arrive at the CEO's office.

"She's a witch," one of the underlings downstairs said to Charlene when we came in. "She'd boil her own grandmother and have her for breakfast."

The witch, sitting behind a mammoth desk, looks up and smiles a white-toothed, professional smile that reaches wide but never makes it past her cheeks.

Charlene lays the debt-collecting letter on the desk, open-faced. "Can you tell me why I received this?" Slowly she reaches into her jeans pocket and pulls out a stack of bills, counts out three twenties and a five. "After I paid my health insurance and utility bills, this is what I have left. It has to last me the rest of the month. Isn't that right, Luci?"

I nod. I also know she made a good-sized payment on a niece's hospital bill from her fifteen-hundred-dollar social security check. I don't think it quite honest for her to give money away and then claim she barely has enough to reach around, but I remain silent, not divulging that information nor my opinion.

The CEO, smiling, talks about good business and necessary business practices. She says if Charlene has been making regular payments, however small, the letter was a mistake. She apologizes and says it is the fault of whomever takes care of these things downstairs. Her eyes are direct and tired. "I'll dispose of this," she says, picking up the letter and depositing it into the trash can.

Charlene smiles, satisfied. "You're not a witch."

"What?"

"You're a nice lady. You're not as bad as they made you out to be downstairs."

"Tell them that, would you?"

"I will."

Slowly, Charlene pushes herself up from her chair. I stand too and crook my arm for her to hold, and we totter out the door and back down the long hallway. A lady, probably one of the office workers, walks toward us.

"She's not so bad!" Charlene crows. "She's a nice lady."

The lady looks confused for a moment, then smiles. "Thank you!"

We pass the one-time cells of the Servite sisters and continue down the stairway, Charlene clinging to the rail and lumping down one step at a time. We step past the beautiful old chapel with stained-glass windows and past the statue of Mary beside the door.

Charlene tells me a story of school days that pastes itself to my imagination like a photo: nuns in black habits, a brick school building, a statue of Mary, a green spring day, and children kneeling in a circle around the statue, praying.

I am angry when I hear this. Angry.

"It's just what happened," Charlene says.

But I feel that Yahweh Elohim, the alone God, has been desecrated.

Once, long ago, a mountain shook and thundered and smoked, and the people were afraid. From a thick cloud on the mountain, God told Moses to tell the people: You shall have no other gods besides me ... You shall not bow down to them, nor serve them: for I, Yahweh Elohim, am a jealous God.

"How could the nuns teach something that goes against the Bible?" I ask.

"We didn't read from the Bible," Charlene says. "I never heard the nuns read from the Bible."

The nuns did teach morals, though, and the Ten Commandments.

According to Charlene, they resented her because she was good at everything she did—quick in her schoolwork and athletic enough to beat the boys at their own games at recess time. Since she had to do the morning chores on her grandpa's farm, she'd take the shortcut to get to school on time. Every morning, she'd pray for her guardian angel to be with her, and then run over the train trestle that crossed the Flambeau River.

Several weeks later, Charlene again brings up the subject of praying to Mary. Apparently, she's been working it over in her mind and wants me to understand something.

"When we were young, the nuns taught us to pray to Mary."

She leans forward, elbows on the table, speaking in the slow-voiced rhythm of her stories. Nibaa sets a chew toy on my knee and stares up with black liquid eyes, body poised and stiff, begging me to throw.

"Praying to Mary was part of learning about God and Jesus," Charlene says. "That was not wrong for me to do. But I remember the neighbors had a dog that would follow me to school every day. I got so sick and tired of that dog following me that one time when I was walking over the trestle and it was behind me, I turned around and yelled, 'Go home!'" She straightens her body with her words, her voice growing harsh and emphatic. "And then when it didn't leave, I kicked it in the stomach as hard as I could. The dog went sailing through the air and landed in the river below. I don't know what happened to it." She pauses, her voice quieting. "That was wrong."

I nod, and we are both silent, the story hanging between us. Sitting across the table from this dark-eyed Ojibwe storyteller, I comprehend something for the first time.

God is not bound. He does not limit his talking—that quiet, piercing voice I know—to a small group of people who happen to be born in the correct time and place and religion.

I've been concerned for Charlene, worried that if she hasn't prayed the proper prayer in the proper way, she can't truly be born again. In the same way, I feel bad for the people who pray to Mary. I know that doing so is wrong, the worship of a false god, and think no one who prays to Mary can possibly be right with God or go to heaven unless they repent.

But as an innocent child, Charlene prayed to Mary because she thought it was part of learning about God and Jesus. In her young mind, she was not worshipping Mary, but worshipping God.

And in the first clear color of understanding, I know God is equal in all nations to all people. Whether to child, adult, simple-minded or learned, he speaks in the simple straightforward language of conscience. Maybe in the same way Charlene speaks, leaning forward at the table, talking sense.

Maybe I've been envisioning a heart like a Ping-Pong ball, bounced to the side of "saved" or "unsaved" on the paddle of the correct religious belief. But a heart is more substantial than that, more like soil, like crumbly rich stuff with worm droppings and leaf bodies and mold mixed into it. "Ye shall know them by their fruits," Jesus said. The measure of soil—or of a heart—is what it produces.

I know that Charlene, like all of us, has committed many sins—impure thoughts and selfish actions for which God holds her accountable. But praying to Mary was not one of them. As a child, she worshiped God and kicked a dog. One was right, the other wrong.

In preaching mode one day, I tell Charlene, "Everybody likes to say they love God. But if they're not doing the things he says, it's only words. If somebody really loves him, you can tell it by their life."

"Would you say I love God?"

I hesitate. "Yes ..." I hear the tiny inflection of question in my voice.

Her eyes grow moist.

I wish I had given a more positive "Yes." I didn't know the question was so important to her. Now I wonder if the tears are relief that I said yes or hurt because I doubted.

Charlene's relationship with God is something I don't fully understand. She did not grow up as I did, with Bible verses and strong moral values, but she holds a deep sense of him, a connection that goes back to childhood.

"I've always loved God," she told me once. "I might not have talked about it, but I loved him."

She holds also a deep respect for his commandments and told me how the owners of the factory where she worked once told everyone to come in on Sunday to fill a large and important order on time. Even though they would be given double pay, she refused. God had said, "Remember the Sabbath day to keep it holy," and keep it she would. Instead, she came in Monday, hours early, and worked like a squirrel on steroids, even enlisting the help of the janitor to get her part of the order filled.

I sense in her a deep hunger for God, the same sort of hunger I feel in my own heart. I always thought a relationship with God must be taught, but, watching Charlene, I begin to think differently. Now I wonder if every person in the world has—as I do and as Charlene does—a connection with God that is private and below everything.

This is not to say everyone honors the seed, or nurtures it, but maybe, for everyone, the seed is there.

Charlene's life now is a constant battle against pain and loneliness. Often, she is angry. "Why does he do this to me?" she asks over and over again when the pain grabs her. And not knowing what else to say, I murmur, "I love you," and other soothing phrases, over and over again.

At other times, she talks of accepting God's will. She keeps a framed picture hanging above her dresser of Jesus with his hands clasped and body bowed across a rock in the garden of Gethsemane.

"I told God, 'Not my will, but thine be done,'" she says once, her eyes moist. "Even if it means losing Luci."

One day as we walk out of the reservation pharmacy, her hand in the crook of my elbow, we see that a light, steady rain has begun. Walking down the ramp to the parking lot, Charlene lifts her face.

"We gladly accept whatever you send," she says into the rain.

I like that. I will try to remember.

One Monday before running errands in town, we go to Dairy Queen and sit in a corner booth, Charlene with a hot fudge sundae and I with a dipped cone. Licking my ice cream, I watch Charlene eating hers. I often watch people when I think they aren't aware of it, but with Charlene, I watch deliberately, wanting her to know. Watching feels like a sort of power—a way to keep my personality intact and in control in face of the grip her psyche holds on mine.

She takes a bite of her hot fudge sundae, the plastic spoon filled mostly with chocolate sauce and only a little ice cream.

"That bite is all chocolate," I say, in a voice intended to convey humor.

Charlene is not amused. Without uttering a word, she stands up, shoves her hot fudge sundae in my direction, and marches out of the building. She always moves fastest when she's mad.

I take a few bites of the sundae—I hate to see it go to waste—and follow her out of the building. She's halfway out to the car by the time I catch up to her.

"You can take me home."

"What are you so mad about?" I ask as we drive back toward her house.

"You don't have to criticize the way I eat my ice cream."

"I wasn't criticizing. I was just observing. You don't have to get so mad about such a little thing."

"It wasn't little to me."

I drop her off at her house and do not offer to help her inside, secretly glad because now I can go home. I have other things to do.

The following day, as usual, I visit on my supper break. It's been a busy shift, though, and I arrive at her house forty-five minutes later than usual. By the time I walk in the door, Charlene sits sullen and angry because she thought I wasn't coming.

Two days later, I arrive to mow her yard as we've planned. Charlene sits on her recliner, her face groggy bright from her nap. "You won't have much time to mow," she grumbles.

"I have an hour and fifteen minutes."

"Oh. I looked at the clock wrong."

After mowing the lawn, I get the dandelion digger from the garage and dig dandelions, an exercise of which Charlene approves but I consider pointless. But anything is preferable to going inside the house and facing that grump.

I enter briefly right before work, perch on the rocking chair across from her for a total of two minutes and chatter about the mower and the dandelions. "I love you," I say when I get up to go.

"I think you must. Because you do things for me, and you don't talk back to me."

I promise to be back the next day around two thirty, after my morning shift. But the next day, I arrive at Charlene's an hour later than planned. I'd forgotten about our mandatory employee meeting and hadn't counted on a Walmart stop I needed to make. Once again, she sits stiff and sullen.

I ignore her sullenness and slather silence with cheerfulness. By the time I've finished my tardiness explanation, her face has eased a little.

"Sorry I'm so grumpy. I had a long day, and I'm tired."

I've already decided I won't hang around long if she's grumpy. "I'll go now, so you can take a nap."

Sharp regret leaps into her eyes, and, softened by the regret, I lean over and kiss her cheek. The hardness leaves her eyes, and her face relaxes. A kiss is rare.

We continually play games with each other. I come in happy and glowing, and Charlene, with a build-up of impatience and a quick jerk of temper, snaps about misunderstood directions or some clumsy mistake. Afterward, when I grow sullen and quiet, she becomes warm and rich with kindness.

She makes me angry more often than I've ever been made angry before. I try to repress the anger. I don't want to give her the pleasure of knowing her effectiveness, but more than anyone else I've ever known, Charlene knows the art of making me mad.

There is no civility about her.

When we visit my family or go out to eat with my friends, she makes snide comments to the others, making fun of what she considers my quirks. This doesn't anger me.

It hurts.

I wonder when I fell so in love that Charlene has such power over me. And why? What is there to love about her?

Charlene asks the same question. Sometimes when I say, "I love you," she says, "I don't understand why."

I don't understand it either. I try to hold myself separate, like a bridge coolly spanning a river, but Charlene has the ability, with her tiny fingers, to loosen the mortar that holds the bricks in place, to tumble the bridge into pieces, and to drop me into the water, splashing and mad.

Maybe it's because she says things other people don't say.

"I'd rather fight than switch," she tells me one day.

I look at her blankly.

"I'd rather fight than switch my way of thinking."

I would rather open my mind to a new way of thinking, but I have never been made to feel threatened, never been made to feel my identity is less than another's, never been made to feel I am forced to conform. If I had been, I admit to myself, I would fight, and fight hard.

Probably all people are like this. They just don't state their motivations as blatantly as Charlene. Most people, when fighting, pretend to have reason.

One day, Charlene yells one time too many. She doesn't apologize—she seldom does—but she tries to make it up afterward by being warm and gracious.

But this wound—or maybe it's a gathering of wounds—digs deeper than the others. This time I cannot forgive.

I go away to work, as I always do, and as I walk the nursing home hallways and answer call lights, outwardly smiling and attentive, I wonder, *Why?*

Why should I keep trying with Charlene? Why continue to be her friend? There seems no earthly reason. She is always angry and always taking her anger out on me. She has nothing to give but a pathetic love I don't need. She's not a whole person, but a twisted half one, with words like fire and ice. There is something hard in her, something incomprehensible to me. I hoped for change, for a softening, but Charlene won't change for me, ever. She told me so.

And why, why, why should I love her? What earthly reason is there when she hurts me like this?

On my fifteen-minute break, I sit on the dark nursing home patio and pull out the Bible I always carry to work—a pocket-sized maroon Bible with worn binding and a black shaved spot where I put a sticker once. I page to familiar words and peer at them in the dim light shining through glass patio doors. "Charity suffereth long, and is kind; charity envieth not ... is not easily provoked, thinketh no evil; rejoiceth not in iniquity, but rejoiceth in the truth; beareth all things, believeth all things, hopeth all things, endureth all things."

I've heard the words in sermons a hundred times, along with the accompanying message: love is not only an emotion but a choice.

I wonder now about this choice and the power of it. Can love—God's kind of love—really conquer anything?

"Charity never fails."

Deep in my heart, down below the anger, I believe.

But the anger remains and will not go away. It's rooted deep, all the little angers and little hurts like rootlets entwined into one knobby mass.

"Dear God, help me to forgive Char," I pray.

I repeat my prayer over and over the next day as I walk through shops with my mom and sisters. At the Lunchbox—a combined gift shop and restaurant—I find a small, faceless figurine on a shelf. A woman in white, holding her heart. *Abundant Love,* the card beside the figurine reads. Something inside me whispers, "Buy this for Charlene."

I take the figurine to the counter and pay for it and realize with joy that the anger has gone. My heart is weeping and broken, but my spirit is free.

That afternoon, on my way to work, I stop at Charlene's house while she is at dialysis and leave the gift on the table with a note.

As always, I come back on my supper break for a quick visit. We talk trivialities.

"Thank you for the little gift," Charlene says, after a while. She tries to say it naturally, but tears move to the backs of her eyes and hang there a moment, unshed.

"You're welcome," I say.

So she knows, too, what the gift meant.

In her witch voice, Charlene asks me one day, "Who cares if I go to hell?" her face and eyes worn after dialysis, body stiff as she waits for pain to pass. "I'm living in hell already. What would be the difference?"

"Yes, and would you want to go on living like this forever?" I hear the passion in my voice. I hate her pain, hate that I cannot stop it.

"What makes you think God thinks I'm good enough to let me into heaven?"

I've grown tired of her endless skepticism—always questioning, always baiting. Haven't we discussed this very thing, or alluded to it, again and again?

"You know what I would say to that."

Her face closes and anger leaps into her eyes. "Fine. If that's the way you want to be." She looks away to the bird feeder outside the window.

In silence, we watch two sparrows attack the seed, flecks spitting from their beaks.

"I'm sorry," I say, after a minute. "I just thought you already knew."

"I really don't know, Luci."

"You can't be good enough to get to heaven. The only way any of us will go there is through the blood of Christ."

She nods, face lightening, genuine relief in her eyes.

I know Charlene is working through questions about God—sorting memories and regrets—but she is her own person, unabashed and alone. I have no desire to intrude.

In her methodical, determined way, she continues to read three chapters a day from the Bible. When she's finished the New Testament, she asks, "Do you think it would be okay if I read it again?"

"Yes, of course."

"I haven't read all the way through the Old Testament yet, and that's why I ask. I'm afraid I'll die before I get through the Book. I want to finish before I die, but I like the New Testament best."

After her second reading of Matthew, she tells me, "I think they were the most beautiful words I ever read."

Sometimes she asks questions like, "Where in the Bible does it say fornication is wrong?" or "What does it mean to repent?" or "Do you think God could forgive a murderer?" She asks that question more than once.

JULY 2012

One hot summer afternoon, I slip through Charlene's door, grinning. "Hello!"

Without looking up from her solitaire game, she says, "Hello."

"Hello, Nibaa." Nibaa jumps and yips excitedly at my knees. She's gotten her summer haircut, and her shortened fur is soft as chick's down.

I sit down across from Charlene, who still won't look at me. I don't know why. Maybe because she didn't see me yesterday. Sometimes when she hasn't seen me for a while, she doesn't look right away.

After half a minute, she does look up and smiles at me, her face gentle.

I love her gentle. Sometimes she is lava—fiery and aggressive. But gentle, she is a smooth lake at twilight, a trace of pink just above the water.

Nibaa is still jumping, wild against my legs.

"Nibaa!" Charlene scolds.

"Should I tie her out for a while?"

"Go ahead."

I stoop to attach Nibaa to her leash.

"And when you go out, look in the front seat of my car. You'll find a frame there with words. Bring that in."

I chain Nibaa to the lilac bush in the front yard and go to the garage, where I find a wall hanging propped in the passengers' seat of Charlene's car. Its frame is a nondescript cheap wood, the tan-colored paper it holds rippled with dampness, spots of brown glue along one edge. Its words are magnificent. I feel as though I'm reading the Magna Carta in original document.

> Go placidly amid the noise and haste, & remember what peace there may be in silence. Speak your truth quietly & clearly ... Neither be cynical about love; for in the face of all aridity & disenchantment it is perennial as the grass ... You are a child of the universe, no less than the trees & the stars; you have a right to be here. And whether or not it is clear to you, no doubt the universe is unfolding as it should ... With all its sham, drudgery, & broken dreams, it is still a beautiful world ...

At the bottom of the frame is a postscript: *Found in Old Saint Paul's Church, 1692.*

I carry it inside. "This is really neat, Char."

"Do you think you'd be allowed to hang it in your room?"

I laugh at her question, my free laugh, and Charlene smiles, her face wrinkling upward and relaxing, eyes shining. "I guess I can if I want to."

"Or maybe you don't want it."

"Yes, I want it. I like it."

Her wrinkles deepen, and she dips her head in satisfaction.

"Is it too hot to paint?" she asks then.

With great anticipation, she is preparing for her family reunion, and I've promised to paint the porch. Mary already painted the kitchen, covering the smoke-yellowed walls with blue the color of the sky—Charlene's favorite color.

"It's not too hot," I say. "Painting won't take me long."

I take the small can of porch paint outside and stoop, painting first the small porch, then the steps, dipping my brush directly from the can. The sun shines hot on the back of my neck, and in a couple of minutes I am sweaty. A neighbor walks down the street and waves.

"Hot day for painting!"

"Yes," I say.

When I've finished, I take the paint can inside and pound the lid shut. "I can do another coat in a couple of days," I tell Charlene.

She nods and hands me a tall glass of lemonade. "This is for you."

Charlene doesn't do things for me very often because she is frail and limited in her abilities, but when she does, she gives it the feel of a sacred ritual. She offers her gifts delicately, with intent and love.

I sip the lemonade. Watery.

"Does it taste like lemonade?"

"Yes, thank you." I keep drinking, and below the melting ice cubes, the beverage is delicious. Best lemonade I've ever had.

I bring Nibaa in from outside and pick up my purse from the table.

"Goodbye, Char."

She stands to give me a hug—gentle and quick this time. My chin fits just over her shoulder, my arms just under her shoulder bones.

"I just love my kitchen painted in this blue."

I nod. "Well, I love you."

She laughs. "I love you too."

Her face wears the hooded look of the baby sparrow in its nest, mouth open. I think that she is missing me already, that she'll be lonely when I'm gone. This need of hers for companionship hangs in the air, brushes my skin, but neither of us mention it.

At home, I research my Magna Carta-ish document and find that it was not really discovered in a church in 1692 but was written by Max Ehrmann in 1927. He gave it the Latin title "Desiderata."

Things desired.

I take in a few hours of Charlene's family reunion. Since I've become acquainted with some of the family and feel comfortable with them, I enjoy myself. The reunion is Charlene's moment of glory. She smiles, makes jokes and conversation, and is a prime bidder in the family auction. She's dressed up for the occasion, moving from blue jeans to slacks and exchanging her simple summer shirt for a pin-striped cream with a ruffle around the neck. I know about the careful decision, know she chose long sleeves to hide her thin arms with their purple bruises.

She's lost another couple of pounds recently, bringing her down to ninety-four when she's weighed after dialysis. With a hammer and nail against the workbench in the garage, I pound another notch into her belt and tell her she'd better keep eating.

"I'm doing my best," she says.

When the family disperses after the reunion, Charlene's oldest sister Wanda stays another week, visiting the siblings who live in the area. Ten years older than Charlene, Wanda is everything Charlene is not. Friendly, gracious, conversational, and a picture of California good health and activity.

Charlene, Wanda, and I visit the two quilt shops in town. I don't often enter this arena. Walking through the maze of color-coordinated fabrics, past buttons, spools of thread, do-it-yourself kits, and brightly printed quilts and purses, I feel like Gretel in a fairy-tale candy house.

Wanda looks for fabric for a quilt she is working on. In California, when she's not manicuring flower gardens in her sub-development, she makes quilts, using vintage fabrics and hand stitching for authenticity.

"At the reunion," Charlene announces to Wanda across bolts of fabric near the counter, "John was going around bad-mouthing everyone else's children, and I went up to him and looked him in the eye and said, 'I forgive you, John.' He said, 'Why?' and I said, 'For being such a swine.'"

Embarrassment rises in me. Why does Charlene have to bring up family squabbles right in front of the fabric store proprietor?

"Yeah, he does run people down quite a bit, doesn't he?" Wanda says.

"I love him, but I just don't like him."

After the fabric shops, we eat lunch at the Back Door.

While Charlene chooses the roast pork, and I choose the broasted chicken, Wanda choses a garden salad. The choice fits her. It fits California and flower gardens and the restoring of quilts. She keeps the conversation going nicely, chattering on and on in pleasant, well-mannered tones.

Somewhere in the conversation, Charlene brings up Black people.

"All they do is pop out babies for their grandmas to take care of and the government to feed. If it was me, I would just throw them all into the river. Let the salmon eat them."

Her strident and obnoxious voice carries clearly to the other tables. Again, I feel embarrassed, and I think Wanda does too.

"There's plenty of poor White trash who live on welfare just as much as the Black people," Wanda says.

"Would salmon eat a Black person?"

"I don't think so," Wanda says, as though this is a normal conversational topic. "But maybe they would. We put pork chops into our pond and the fish ate them, bones and all. They eat almost anything."

I want to laugh. Wanda must be as flummoxed as I feel.

But she rallies quickly and talks in a light, conversational tone about her vacation to Mexico. There she observed the poverty of the people and how hard they worked just to make a living.

"I don't like when I hear people calling them dirty Mexicans. I don't like when people are prejudiced against other people just because they don't understand them."

I think Wanda missed her calling in flowers and quilts. She was born to be a diplomat. I shoot Charlene a meaningful look across the table. She smiles at me, her face radiating that expression she gets of almost-amusement, and of course, I cannot keep from smiling back.

Charlene mentions Black people again a little bit later, using the N word as their title. This time Wanda is ready for her.

"I don't think you should call them that. That's just like saying dirty Mexican."

"Well, what should I call them?"

"Call them Black people. I don't think anyone who's had the experiences we've had should treat other people in a derogatory way. Remember how they used to treat us because we were half-Indians? I remember somebody throwing stones at me, and I went home and asked Mom why, and she said some people just don't understand."

I shoot another meaningful look at Char, writing agreement into every atom of my face.

The conversation moves on. Wanda talks about a documentary she watched on the Hutterites, a "plain people" who, like the Mennonites, trace their heritage to the Anabaptists. The most distinctive tenet of Hutterite belief is their practice of communal living.

"The women, in the spring, kick off their shoes and go right out and work in the garden in their bare feet," Wanda says. "Then they wash them before they go in the house. It reminded me of Mom, what she'd used to do. It reminded me of the Midwest."

I do that very thing every summer and marvel that what I had considered ordinary, someone else considers old-fashioned and memorable.

"The women of the colony asked for a motorized cart to haul their garden things in," Wanda says. "But the men decided against it. They said the women didn't need a cart—that it was too fancy for them, even though they themselves drove big top-of-the-line machinery in the fields."

"Yes," Charlene says, "her grandpa used to drive me to dialysis, and I really got into it with him. He'll never forget me."

"My grandpa isn't like that!" I snap.

"I know that now," she says, "but that's how I thought he was back then." She looks pleased, as she always does when she gets an untamed reaction from me.

"We shouldn't be prejudiced against people just because they're different," Wanda says again.

The next day, Charlene has rethought her approach. "Wanda was right," she tells me. "It was in poor taste for me to talk about Black people the way I do. People don't like it."

"People don't like it? What do you suppose God thinks about it?"

She looks as disgruntled as if mud has been rubbed in her face but holds grimly to her humility.

"I suppose he doesn't like it either. I won't do it again."

When I stop in at Charlene's a few days later, Wanda is there for a final visit, talking in her pretty, nonstop voice. The lines of Charlene's face are relaxed, and she is smiling and gracious in a way I have seldom experienced. They sit at the kitchen table, eating chocolate sundaes from Dairy Queen.

"I had to cook us supper," Charlene says.

"Are you sure you didn't have to churn it up in a churn?"

She smiles, her eyes sparkling.

I go outside to mow the lawn. By the time I've finished, Wanda has gone, and I go inside and sit where she sat, across from Charlene at the table.

The lines of her face are still relaxed, peaceful in the mellow evening light. "I told Wanda how I'm reading the Bible," she says, "and how I find so many interesting things there, and so much I don't understand. She says she has no interest in reading the Bible."

I hear the wonder in her voice and step into her mood. "Isn't that funny?"

"Yes. We were all brought up in the same family, all brought up as Catholics. Wanda said she doesn't believe in heaven or hell. 'Doesn't it matter whether you've been a good person or a bad person?' I asked her. And she said, 'No. I think we all just go to a different plane.' 'Then where does God live?' I asked. 'Well,' Wanda said, 'from what I remember in catechism class, God lives everywhere.' And I didn't have any answer or question for that."

We sit in silence, looking out the window at the sunlight stretching across the grass.

"God does answer prayer," Charlene says. "Sondra gave her boyfriend the boot."

Sondra is Mary's daughter, Charlene's great niece.

"Is that what you were praying for?"

"Yes. Max ran over Sondra, took over her life. Sondra is like her mom. She needs her space. If I had the chance, I'd kill him. I told them all that. I'd just kill him. Somebody said it wouldn't be worth it, and I said, 'What do I have to lose? Do I want to live a few more pain-filled years?'"

I am nettled. "That wouldn't be worth it. Pain-filled years and years of burning. That would be stupid."

She looks pleased. "Well, I'd do it anyway to prove my point. I told them that's why the boys never wanted to take me to a gun show. They knew if I got a hold of a gun, I'd kill somebody. And they said that's probably true."

"God loves Max as much as he loves you."

"I suppose so. But I would never treat someone the way he did. Does that make him as good as me?"

"Oh, you wouldn't, would you?" I remember all the times I've heard Charlene tell people off, all the times I've felt myself manipulated or run over.

She seems oblivious to my sarcasm. "No, I wouldn't. We think we have problems, but think about the problem God has with Max. That baby Sondra is carrying, will God make him normal, or less than perfect?"

I glare at her.

"What do you think?" she demands.

"I think someone who claims to follow Jesus Christ and believe in him has no business talking like that. It's like slapping him in face."

"Oh, come on, Luci. It's not that bad, me not liking him."

"I mean you killing him ... but maybe your family all know you're not serious."

I wait, half expecting her to protest that yes, she really is serious. Charlene doesn't say anything, just sits observing me with an interested, but not unpleasant, look on her face.

"You want your family to follow God and believe in Jesus, and then you talk like that. They're not going to listen to anything you say!"

"They don't listen anyway." She waves a hand dismissively, and I change the subject.

"Should I work on that butter churn lid?"

Charlene owns several butter churns, the glass-jar, tabletop variety, which she hopes to sell to an antique dealer. One of the churns has a lid that is too large, and she recently suggested I wrap the inside rim of the lid with duct tape to make it fit properly.

I am skeptical of such redneck meddling with an antique, but being myself, do not mention my skepticism.

"Bring it out here," Charlene says, "and we'll do it together."

I bring out the churn and set it on the table while she smokes a cigarette.

As I work on the lid, she is quiet, watching me wrap, and I grow uneasy in the silence. I try to make conversation and think of the reunion. We haven't discussed it much, and I know how important it was to her.

"What was your favorite part of the reunion?"

She thinks a moment before answering. "I don't know that I had a favorite part. I enjoyed all of it. I liked all the laughter. There was a lot of laughter."

"You're good at having fun, aren't you?"

Charlene nods. Smiles. "Whatever happened to laughing so hard your belly hurts?" Memory big in her eyes, she tells me a story from her youth.

"I remember when we were younger, Wanda came home for a visit and decided to go into town. She asked if any of us needed anything. Mary piped up and said, 'You can get me a bottle of wine.' Mary was all of thirteen and never drank wine.

"'What kind do you want?' Wanda wondered.

"'What's a good kind?' Mary asked Mom.

"'Well,' Mom said. 'At Christmas time I like to have a glass of Mogen David.'

"'Okay,' said Mary. 'Get a bottle of Mogen David, and then Mom can have some with us.'

"When Wanda came back from town, she had four bottles of Mogen David. Why did she get so much? Mom wondered.

"'Well,' said Wanda. 'If you bought one bottle, you could get three other bottles for half price. So if I got the three other bottles, I was getting the fourth one free.'

"'Oh, okay,' we said, and between the three of us—Wanda and Mary and I—we drank those four bottles of wine. We sat there laughing and getting sillier and sillier until Mom said, 'Well, girls, I think it's time for you to go up to bed.'

"We went up the stairs, laughing the whole way. We kept falling and tripping over our feet and couldn't make it up the steps, so we decided the best way would be to crawl. We crawled into our beds—just mattresses on the floor, and one of us would say something or one of us would fart and we'd all be laughing again.

"Mom called up the stairs, 'Girls, quiet down. Do I need to come up there?'

"'Okay, Mom,' we said, and something struck us funny and we laughed some more. Mom wasn't the type to hit us. She just wasn't that kind of mom.

"'Oh, I'm gonna be sick,' Mary said.

"'Don't be sick here. Don't get it on the bed. Go puke in the toilet,' we told her.

"Well, Wanda decides she's getting up to help her and she cracks her head on the edge of the bed, and I'm yelling, 'Mary, Mary, don't be sick yet. We gotta see if Wanda's hurt. She was getting up to help you and she hurt her head.'

"Well, it just cracked open the skin pretty good, nothing too serious. But after a while our bellies hurt, and it wasn't necessarily from being drunk. It's because we were laughing so hard. Our mouth and our cheeks hurt, the skin was stretched tight over them. I think that's the last time I ever laughed that hard."

I smile, then gasp, remembering something I haven't told her. I open my mouth to explain and close it again. Now is probably not a good time.

"What?" Charlene asks.

"I just thought of something, but it isn't very fun ... a boy I know. He died this morning in a logging accident. Sorry, I know death isn't a very nice thing to talk about. It's just that I have never known a year with so many deaths as this one."

Her eyes deepen, hold regret and sadness.

I continue wrapping duct tape around the butter churn lid—around, around, around. "I'll be dreaming about this tonight."

She smiles, but the sparkly look in her eyes has disappeared. I regret stealing her happy mood with my scolding and my talk of death.

"I love you," I say.

She doesn't answer, and I feel stupid. I go back to wrapping, feeling self-conscious now.

"I'll never understand that."

I look up. "Why not?"

"A crotchety old bag."

"You're not a crotchety old bag. You're funny and interesting and full of love."

She looks away, hiding the crying that springs into her eyes. "Well, I'd better take my pills. I just keep sitting here and forgetting to take them."

She gets up and steps slowly toward the cupboard for her pill box.

I continue wrapping—around, around, around.

Several weeks later, I sit in Charlene's darkened living room and hear her say that Max is dead. I am staying overnight when she tells me. She sits cross and tight in her recliner, and I perch in the rocking chair, my backpack on the floor beside me.

Charlene never liked Max, and neither did Taylor, Sondra's daughter. Sondra thought he might be the right one for her and got pregnant with his child, but according to Charlene, Max took too much too quickly. He took over Sondra's house and their relationship. When he proposed to Sondra, she said no. Now he is dead.

"Max went to see Sondra last night," Charlene says, "but she was going out and couldn't talk. So he went into town and got drunk. Afterward, he fell down a stairway, hit his head, and died."

I cry.

Divorce, rape, adultery, murder, drunkenness—all these things have happened in Charlene's family, and, through her stories, all these things have become real to me only this year. The stories run together in my mind as one immense soggy swamp of sorrow and sin.

"Why are you crying? You don't know him," she says.

"I'm sorry. I don't know why I'm crying. It's just ... I never knew people were so unhappy."

Charlene smiles a little. She seems to understand.

Then, she becomes grim as she talks about her sister. Mary, it seems, is all in a stew, worried about Sondra and busy in the process of comforting her.

"I have no idea why." Charlene speaks with the harsh grating voice I don't like. "She didn't like the guy, and now he's dead. Why should she need comfort?"

I glare at her, hating her harshness and letting my disrespect show in my eyes. I have done this before with Charlene, trying to abash her without words. Sometimes she backs down.

But tonight she calls me out. "Now you look at me like you hate me. What are you thinking?"

"I don't hate you." I pull my eyes quickly back to myself, make them distant and soft.

We cobble words over the high wall of anger between us, Charlene stiff and unreachable, I distant.

"I'm going to bed," she says finally.

"I'm gonna go outside for a while."

I sit in the blackness of the side yard, bow my head to the ground, elbows in the cool grass, and pray. The stars above me look faded because of the city lights, not bright as they do at home on the farm. Some kids pass on the sidewalk across the street, and I realize that to them walking down the street at night is normal and mundane. I have never lived in a town and have the uneasy feeling there might be a stabbing around any corner, that there will be wild partying and drugs trading hands.

The boys pass, and my thoughts about them. I stare at the faded stars, pray for a long time, let my mind circle through limbo. I regret glaring at Charlene and wonder why I feel no sympathy for her, only distance and anger. The anger lessens in the darkness, but not the dislike. I go into the house, finally, and fall asleep.

The next morning, Charlene tries to get us back on even ground. "I was thinking, and I realized I've lost my sense of humor. The Indians believed in laughter, and I've forgotten how to laugh."

I wasn't angry with her for lack of laughter, but for lack of compassion. But I appreciate her effort to make amends.

"You tell me why I should feel sorry for Sondra," she says. "Explain to me why Sondra is hurting."

"Well, if it was me, and I had a boyfriend, and I sent him away and he went into town and got drunk and died, I would feel like it was my fault. And even if Sondra and Max had broken up, they had been together for quite a while, and there was still that relationship. It would still hurt that he died. And he was the father of her baby."

She tips her head. "I need people to tell me these things. I don't know because it never happened to me."

I love visiting Charlene best on Sunday mornings. We talk in the quiet about personal things neglected during the weekly shopping, weeding, and mowing. We talk about the Bible on Sundays. We talk about God.

One Sunday, I arrive to find Charlene on the phone. She has not yet taken her shower and wears her light summer robe, her arm through only one of the sleeves. The other sleeve dangles uselessly from her shoulder, exposing her right breast and just above it, the catheter port used for dialysis.

She has already taped plastic baggies over the gauze-wrapped port and the dressing that surrounds it, since it's important for this invasive and infection-prone opening into her body to stay clean and dry.

While she showers, I doze in her recliner, enjoying the rare feel of sitting where she always sits.

When Charlene comes out of the bathroom, she has the robe on again, the sleeve still dangling. In spite of her care and the plastic baggies, a corner of the dressing has gotten wet and will have to be changed.

She sits down at the table, and I sit beside her and begin to pull off the sticky square of cloth tape, pressing down the skin as I pull to try to keep it from hurting. The skin is ivory colored, brittle, bruised. It lifts an inch from her chest as I pull, giving me more an idea of Egyptian papyrus than of living flesh. I finish pulling the wetted half of the tape and find that the dry part is worse, sticking to her chest like fly paper on hair. I stop.

"I can't do this. I'm afraid I'll hurt you."

She finishes pulling the tape.

I lift the old gauze squares from her chest. I can see where the catheter port dives up under the skin—can see the tiny, dried blood clot at the entry point and the finger length of tube that lifts the thin chest skin. I can imagine yanking on that tube, imagine how the fragile skin would pop open. The thought makes me wince.

I place new squares of gauze at the entry point, working ever so gently to slip them into the right position, my fingers gentle on her skin, barely touching.

"When I do this myself, I have to do it in front of the mirror, and that's when I use up all my swear words for the week," she says.

I laugh.

"Thank you for doing this."

"I like doing this. It makes me feel like a nurse."

"You're my special little nurse."

I lay the square of cloth tape over the gauze, ever so carefully, and pat it down.

Charlene tells me then about her phone conversation.

"Mary just unloads everything to me. She called at six thirty."

"And that's who you were still talking to when I got here at eight?"

She nods. "She'll talk to me over the phone, but she won't talk to me in person. I don't understand why. I know I intimidate people because people have told me I intimidate them. I don't know why."

I look at how she holds her head up while she talks—a sharp-eyed, sharp-tongued old lady with a spirit and a presence to be reckoned with. She is not the sort to blend into a crowd and be forgotten. She might not know why she intimidates people, but I have no trouble understanding it.

"Maybe I'm like the eagle," she says. "His eagle—I call it his eagle—doesn't smile, and people are intimidated by eagles." Her eyes are lifted and bright. I think that her straight Indian nose could look similar to an eagle's hooked beak, and her flat-planed face and the wide eyebrows with their scattered hairs holds something of the fierceness of an eagle.

"I've never known my brother Emmet to be afraid of anything. But he told me he was sitting in his tree stand one morning, waiting for a deer, when he heard a whoosh, whoosh, whoosh." She lifts her shoulders with each breath, the whooshes emanating from her inner belly like puffs of wind. "It scared him. He had no idea what he'd heard, and then an eagle flew by, no farther than from you to that car." She gestures to my Focus, parked just outside in the driveway. "He was shaking, it scared him so much. He said after that he climbed down out of the tree stand and went into the house."

We are silent, comprehending the story. Charlene has a way of giving simple stories great meaning.

"I'd love to go to church with you this morning, but I know Sondra's hurting and I need to go talk to her. I need to take her the Word of God." I love how she says that, raising her head as though she has a commission.

Her voice lowers. "I don't want to crush her by what I say. I know in my heart that Sondra's friends and Sondra's mom can't heal her. Only God can. I have such faith in him. He controls everything. If you get up and go to the sink to turn on the faucet"—she gestures toward the kitchen sink—"he allows you to do that. But maybe you think I'm going on and on."

"No." I shake my head, mulling over that concept. I believe in the sovereignty of God, or so I've always thought. But I never yet considered it to be only his permission that allows me to turn on the faucet at the kitchen sink.

"I'll pray your talk with Sondra goes well," I say when I leave. "You pray for me, and I'll pray for you."

Charlene nods, her smile stretching across her face. "I always pray for you. I pray that God will keep you safe. I think everyone in the world should have a friend like you."

When I stop by the next day, I ask about the talk with Sondra, curious at her reaction to being taken the Word of God. "What did you tell her?"

"Well, I just asked her, 'Do you believe in God?' She said, 'Yes,' and I told her, 'You'll be okay then.'"

"What did she say?"

She shrugs. "Nothing, really. That was it."

A nice thing about Charlene, in this world of loud and ready answers, when she takes someone the Word of God, she keeps it simple.

OCTOBER 2012

There have been so many hospital visits by now—several bouts of COPD, cataract surgery, routine checkups, and an emergency surgery to replace her dialysis port.

Charlene is tense, snappish, and belligerent every time she enters a hospital, and who can blame her? Hospitals are nothing to her but misery and pain, and she's had to endure so many of them.

When I get off work at eleven one night, I find a message from Mary on my phone. Charlene is in the emergency room in an Eau Claire hospital. She's bleeding internally. I wake up early the next morning and drive the hour to Eau Claire to see her.

"This is it, Luci," she says when I find her in the dialysis unit, blood running in slow flow through tubes. She holds up a limp hand to take mine. "I think I'm going to die, and I'm ready."

I believe her because don't people know these things? She's been listless for the past week.

Mary calls and reassures me. Charlene won't die yet, she says. But what about a nursing home?

Over my dead body, a nursing home! I cannot imagine Charlene without the space and freedom of her own house, without a window for staring at birds. I cannot imagine her with six different girls a week to help her wash up, with scheduled exercises and meals and old-time sing-a-longs.

What I can imagine is this: Charlene sitting alone and tight in a narrow, bedded room, spitting at aides.

I don't think Mary cares.

I am alone with Charlene among strangers. As the first day of her hospitalization stretches to the second, she grows woozy and weak until it seems even she doesn't know me. In my loneliness, the kindness of the nurses is the one thread that connects me to a world of warmth and color and fellowship. Every act means the universe.

That first night, when I am cold, a nurse brings me a heated blanket, and its warmth soaks into my bones. Later, a housekeeper gives me a glass of water, even though it can't be on her list of job responsibilities. A nurse who sees me crying gives me her cell phone number and tells me to call anytime. Another with skin the color of damp earth comes with Charlene's nebulizer, her manner warm and disarming.

I think it ironic that a Black person Charlene despises is caring for her. Or maybe she doesn't. Charlene's racism, like all of her, is riddled with contradictions. She's told me only recently she plans to vote for Obama in the coming election.

She wakes several times in the night, restless and in pain, and once, trying to comfort her, I unwittingly sit on the bed and set off all the alarms. In the early morning, her pain is unbearable, and I push the call button for a nurse.

"What is your pain level on a scale of one to ten?" the nurse asks.

"Twelve, fourteen, sixteen!"

"Do you want a pain pill?"

"Yes."

I know Charlene continually endures pain without complaint and scarcely ever takes pain pills. Her pain must be tremendous.

Later in the morning, after the pain pill kicks in, Charlene tells me in a relieved tone of voice, "I guess I'll be around for a while."

"Sometimes, for your sake, I wish you could go. So you could have relief from all the pain."

She is silent, and I worry I've hurt her.

"But for my sake, I'm glad to have you around."

She smiles and squeezes my hand.

I leave to attend the funeral of my second cousin who died of cancer. When I come back, Charlene is drugged, sleepy, and refusing to eat. A nurse and I, between us, pull words from her about an orange float. But when an aide brings the float up from the cafeteria, she takes only a few bites from the spoon in my hand and then shakes her head.

"Do you want me to stay the night with you again?"

She nods.

As I wait with her through the long afternoon and evening, she starts asking for people, starting with Mary. "I miss my baby sister," she says, and then, "I miss your mom."

I laugh and pat her hand. "Who else do you miss?"

"I miss Luci."

"How can you miss me when I'm right here?"

She gets a big, silly grin on her face. "I just do."

She'll have a birthday soon—her seventy-first—if she survives this bout at the hospital.

"What do you want for your birthday?" I asked her recently.

It was one of her dialysis days, and she sat small and tight, perched in her blue-plaid-covered armchair like a stone washed up in a gully. I thought it was as if someone had lacquered her, had left her bright and sparkling and hard as a child's toy marble. But if you were to touch her, you would find the veneer thin. At a touch, her whole body would wince—blood slamming aortic walls, intestines just so many glass shards set on edge, heart brittle, breaking with every beat.

She considered my question. "I want a new heart," she said. "Make it a turtle heart." She told me the story as she always tells stories—slowly, pausing in places, weighing her words—as though she wore soft beaten leather and sat in the tribal circle.

"One day the neighbor man brought over a turtle and asked me to cook it for him. His wife wouldn't touch it. We chopped off its head and hung it on the clothesline by one of its back legs. That turtle hung there a full hour before it stopped looking for its head. When it finally stopped moving, I called the neighbor man and told him, 'The turtle's dead.'

"He came over and cut the meat out of the shell. We came to the heart and it was still beating. I took it and put it on the kitchen counter. It was a month before that heart stopped beating. The heart had four chambers, and they stopped beating one at a time, one every week, but it was a month before they stopped completely.

"And of course my roommate said,"—here Charlene made her voice high and prissy—"'Oh, gracious! You can't have a beating heart lying on the kitchen counter with the lettuce and the spoons. I can't stand to have it there.' It's not in anybody's way, I told her. Would you rather have it on the kitchen table?"

The turtle heart is like Charlene herself—throbbing and vulnerable and persistent as earthbeat. I know why she wants a new heart. Her own heart has been weak since she had a bout of rheumatic fever as a girl.

But in my mind, her request takes on a broader, symbolic significance. I see Charlene fuse with all aching humanity—with our caught personalities, our trapped sins—asking for a change of heart. Not merely to exchange one throbbing of muscle and capillary for another, but for a rejuvenation of soul.

I want that for us. More than anything, I want it for her.

I've given up worrying whether she is born again or trying to make her so. Charlene knows her Creator, and that's good enough for me. But I see her daily battle with anger, pain, and an indefinable sorrow. I want her to be free.

I want that for all of us.

During our second night at the hospital, I wake from half-sleep to hear Charlene smacking her hand on her bedside table.

Bang, bang, bang. "Can't I get any help around here?"

I sit beside her and talk to her, detangling her matted hair with a comb from my purse. Small sticky pads stick to her chest in various places, monitoring the beating of her heart, and strands of hair have caught beneath them. I clip the strands free with fingernail clippers, also pulled from my purse. I try to teach her to push her call button, worried that since I have to work tomorrow evening, she will spend the night alone. But she is too woozy even to comprehend a call button.

Toward morning, she overflows with words.

"Where's my sister?" she asks, every now and again. "I don't think she wants to see me."

"She does want to see you. I know you love her a lot."

She nods. "I love her. I love Luci too."

She talks quietly, in a multitude of short simple sentences that remind me of a Dick and Jane reader. "Oh, dear," she repeats over and over. "Oh, dear. Oh, dear." In this, her moment of greatest need, her swear words all seem to have left her. The quiet words are worse. They break my heart.

In the morning, when an aide comes to help her get washed up, she wails, "I think I'm going to cry, Luci. I don't want to cry."

"It's okay to cry."

"Is it okay to cry?"

"Yes."

Tears run down my cheeks, but Charlene doesn't cry at all.

While the pretty young aide washes Charlene's face and helps her into her gown, I go into the bathroom to get dressed for the day.

"There's a bug," Charlene says to the aide, over and over. "Did you see him fly by? Look! There he goes!"

"I think it's that floater she always sees because of her macular degeneration," I explain, not wanting her to appear completely crazy.

I'm still in the bathroom, almost finished with my hair, when the aide gathers her things to leave.

"Don't leave me!" Charlene wails.

"Luci's here with you. She's in the bathroom."

I hurry out.

"What were you doing hiding in the bathroom?"

"I wasn't hiding. I put my dress on and got my hair combed for the day."

She starts wailing again. "Do you have to go to work? Don't go to work. Don't leave me. I don't want to die alone."

"Jesus will be with you. Do you trust Jesus?"

She nods. "I love Jesus. But I don't know if Jesus wants to be with me."

"You know how much you love me and how much you love Mary? Put that together and Jesus loves you more than that."

Her eyes grow big.

"He loves you more than you can imagine."

"Wow," she says, as though this is just too much to comprehend.

I smile. "You're my darling."

A young blonde nurse comes in with a student nurse, and Charlene grows upset and talks frantically again of dying. Her delirium scares me. She really might die.

"I don't want to die," Charlene wails, becoming increasingly more upset.

"You're not going to die, Char," I say finally.

She calms immediately.

"We'll take care of you," says the young blonde nurse. Her name tag reads "Megan." She leans over the bed, gentle and smiling. "Can we listen to your heart?"

"Sure," Charlene says, as though this is a great honor. "If you're interested." She tips her head toward me. "She'll be interested."

Both nurses listen, Megan explaining to the student the click of Charlene's artificial heart valves, put there by surgery to replace the fever-damaged ones. When she is done, they straighten to leave.

"Did you hear it?" Charlene asks me.

"No, they didn't give me a chance," I say jovially.

"Ohhhhh." A moan of great disappointment erupts from Charlene.

Megan smiles. "Did you want to listen? You can if you want."

I put the stethoscope in my ears and place the round disc up against Charlene's flat chest. I feel flustered with the nurses standing over me waiting and smiling, and unsure of what I'm supposed to hear. Isn't there supposed to be a clicking sound?

I hear only the irregular fluttering of her heart. Like Charlene, her heart raps out its own uncanny rhythm, weak and wild, and—like the turtle heart she asked for—always fluttering on after what seems to be its final beat.

I don't know if I've heard what I'm supposed to, but I straighten and say I did.

We smile, Charlene, the nurses, and I, in one of those sickly sweet moments I try to avoid. I am suspicious of such moments and label them sentimental and cheesy—like maraschino cherries, too perfect to be real.

But this is Charlene, my sweetheart. Every gland in my body has awakened, throbbing, because she's in trouble. When the nurses are gone, I sit beside her and hold her hand and tell her with my eyes that I love her. I'm not worried about being lesbian now. Let it be.

"Your precious little glasses," she says, her voice like baby talk, eyes caressing.

"I wore them for you because I know you like them."

When an aide comes to take Charlene to dialysis, she is smiling as though this is the happiest day of her life.

I pray she will die. Pray it over and over all through the terrible night and the morning full of delirious words. I want her to be free of pain, and happy. And I want to be free of the responsibility of taking care of her.

But more than anything, I want it to be over. No deeper attachments. Less pain. Sever it now, before it gets too real.

When she leaves for dialysis, I break, crying like rivers, like rainfall, like oceans. I am frantic because I'm supposed to be at work in a few hours, but I don't want to leave.

I want my mom.

My cell phone rings. Mary, on her way to visit.

I try to call Mom, but I've forgotten my charger. My phone beeps mournfully ... again ... again ... and is dead.

And I am weeping in the hallway in front of the nurse's station, asking to use the hospital phone. "I just have to call my mom."

Can you come? I plan to say when Mom picks up, but then I can't say it.

"I don't know if Char is dying," I say instead. "My phone is dead, so I'm using the hospital phone. Mary is coming for a visit. I better go." I can't talk, not here, at the public nurses' station. We hang up, me battling tears.

I go back to Charlene's room and turn on my cell phone again. Two lines of battery. God did a miracle, I think. I am grateful.

I call Mom and sob into the phone. Charlene might be dying, and I have to go to work, but maybe I'll call in and tell them I can't come, because I don't want to leave her.

Dad picks up the phone. "Everything that happens, happens slow," he says, his voice calm, laying out sense. "You go to work like usual because you don't know how much longer this will go on. It could be days."

"But she's scared to be alone at nights." I huff words between sobs, body hunched and shaking. "She doesn't want to die alone."

"You come home. You're overtired and you need to get some sleep. Mom and I will come down after chores and stay overnight with her."

"You will? You don't mind?"

I'm too grateful to protest.

I go up to the dialysis unit to find Charlene. When I see her, I cry again, ashamed to have lost my reserve in public but unable to stop.

Charlene looks at me in wonder, as though this is the first time she's seen me today and she can't figure out why I'm crying.

A nurse with a firm set to her jaw strides past, and I catch her and ask worried questions. She looks at me as though I'm a fool, but my hideous distress softens her enough to put a thin string of kindness into her voice. She pats my shoulder. Charlene is not dying, I realize. This nurse has no thought of it. It's only me who is overwrought.

I bring a metal folding chair and sit beside Charlene. "Mary is coming to see you," I tell her. "And Mom and Dad are coming to visit."

This seems to amaze and honor her. "They are? Why would they come visit me?"

"They'll stay overnight with you, if you need them to."

The nurse comes with questions. "Where are you, Charlene?"

"Hopsil."

"Do you know why you're here?"

"No."

"You've been sick, and now you're having dialysis."

Charlene looks at her with a blank face, not seeming to comprehend.

"You're sick, but I'm here with you," I tell her finally.

"I'm glad you're with me." She looks around. "This place is like a zoo." She points at a nurse walking past. "She's sick." And another one. "She's sick."

"No, they're not sick," I say, unsure whether this is confusion or only sarcasm. "They're nurses."

Mary arrives, bringing her overnight bag. "If she wants me, I'll stay overnight," she promises.

So Mary cares enough. I hadn't trusted that she would.

We walk along with the chair as Charlene is wheeled back to her room, and I tell her goodbye.

She smiles, proud pleasure written across her face. "She's my favoritest," she announces to the room.

"Did you know you're my favoritest too?" I ask, touched by her words.

The thought seems to amaze her. "I am?"

I stagger into work two hours later, tears just below the surface.

I call Mary on my supper break. She reports that Charlene is doing just fine. She doesn't seem confused at all and ate a good supper.

I feel cheated. Charlene wasn't fine when I was with her. It took her capable and practical sister to snap her from crazy land. But mostly, I feel relieved.

So relieved.

I am back at the hospital mid-morning of the following day, refreshed and happy after a good night's sleep.

Charlene is at one hundred percent, has jumped from her fog with the snap of a yo-yo.

Maybe it was the drugs. She took more pain pills and nausea medication within two short days than she normally does for months. Because of her kidney failure, her body has no way until dialysis to rid her bloodstream of the medication.

"Didn't you tell me your parents were coming to visit?" she asks almost as soon as she sees me.

"Yes, they want to come today, since they didn't come yesterday."

She seems as fully amazed this time as she did the first time she heard it.

We wait for the doctor.

He comes, finally. He asks questions, pokes her back so that she gasps, and listens to her heart.

He says she can go home.

I smile. Charlene's face radiates joy.

Mary's face does not.

"I don't think she's well enough to be on her own," she says. "Couldn't she go to a swing bed to recover for a few weeks before she goes home?"

"That might be a good idea," the doctor agrees.

"She likes the hospital in Barron, and she'd be right there close to dialysis."

"What do you think, Charlene?" he asks. "Would you like to go to a swing bed for recovery before you go home?"

Charlene possesses none of her usual fire. "Whatever you want, sister," she says.

What is wrong with her? Why isn't she insisting on going home?

She's remembering how Mary sacrificed to stay with her, and she wants to please her, I think. I know how Charlene waits for Mary's calls, hungers for her visits. She wants to keep the relationship with Mary.

But all the light has died from her eyes.

The doctor tells us that since all the Barron swing beds are full, Charlene's new bed will be in the connected Barron nursing home. "You're only there temporarily," he assures her, "until one of the swing beds opens up."

Mary goes out for a smoke break.

I look at Charlene and drop my eyes, self-conscious now that we're alone. She is watching me.

"What do you think, Luci?"

"I think you're doing the right thing." To be obedient and peaceable is always good, right? That Charlene can be those things awes me and moves me to pity.

She grows restless, her face a screw of trouble, moving her body in the bed impatiently. "I just want to go home. When can I go home?"

My eyes fill with tears. I look away, blink.

"What's wrong?"

"I just wish you could go home."

Her face calms and relaxes. "I love you."

"I love you too, Char."

Mary takes Charlene to Barron and helps her get settled into her temporary room. I am at work and do not observe the uneasy image of pleasantness and cooperation Charlene has become.

The next morning, when I call her, she has changed.

"How are you doing?" I ask. "How was your night?"

"It was terrible." A pause. "Luci, can I ask you to do something for me?"

"Sure. What?"

"I need you to come and take me home."

"But I thought you were going to stay in the swing bed until you finish recovering."

"I'll be fine as soon as I get home. If you don't take me home, I'll walk."

I want to burst into applause.

Pleasantness and cooperation are for the birds.

"I'll take you home, but only if you have a doctor's order. I'm not going to take you home unless he okays it."

I drive the hour to Barron—something I've worried about, this inconvenience of distance. When I arrive, Charlene sits on the edge of a chair in the corner of the room, her back straight and stiff, as sharply out of place as a Warhol perched in a Monet.

"I need to get out of here, Luci."

"Have you told them you want to go home?"

She nods.

"What did they say?"

"The doctor is going to come and talk to me."

"Well, we just need to wait then."

She contains herself, but barely.

The physical therapist arrives to do an assessment, and I watch Charlene totter in slow steps across the room. "I can't put you down as independent while you're here," the therapist says, her voice sympathetic. "That holding on to things—furniture walking, I call it—always makes me nervous."

"I knew I would fail," Charlene says when she is gone.

I laugh at her. "You didn't fail anything. She just means someone needs to help you with walking while you're here, and they'll want you to wear a gait belt. It doesn't mean you can't go home."

She moves impatiently on her chair. "Well, put that thing on me then. Let's go for a walk."

"You mean the gait belt?" I look at the safety belt dangled across the walker that physical therapy provided. "Do you feel like you need to wear the gait belt for safety?"

"No."

"Then there's no reason to use it."

No way am I going to tie her into a gait belt. Gait belts are for old people, like the ones I care for in the nursing home. Charlene isn't old.

We take a slow walk down the hallway, Charlene straight as a stick behind the provided walker, gait belt excluded.

Later, another doctor examines Charlene. She seems friendly, asks a few questions, makes a discreet comment with an almost-wink about family members who like to control things, and says Charlene can go home. After dialysis, of course, and when the nurse has finished the paperwork.

We wait, the hours long, for dialysis to come, and while Charlene is in dialysis, I wait some more. Mona, a pretty dialysis RN with a round face and dark hair, finds me in the waiting room. Charlene talks about her sometimes, calls her a "sweetheart."

"Did you know that Charlene doesn't remember any of her time in the hospital?" she asks. "She remembers going there, and being there afterward, but nothing of the two days she was sick."

So Charlene doesn't remember the long night with me and our special morning together? Only the time Mary spent with her? Again, I feel cheated.

"Keep an eye on her," Mona says, her face concerned.

The day stretches into late afternoon as we wait for the paperwork to be done. Charlene grows more and more impatient—moving up, down, shifting, muttering.

"What is wrong with these people? I'm not waiting any longer. I'm going to leave right now."

"If you want to go home and take care of yourself, act like an adult."

This stricture only calms her minimally. I've never seen her so restless and unable to contain herself.

Finally, the papers. The nurse, the car, the highway.

Charlene trembles in the passengers' seat, her tiny body a limp rag. "Could you stop at a gas station and buy me a pack of cigarettes? I'll pay you back."

Ah, the cigarettes. I forgot about those. No wonder she went crazy there in the hospital room. No wonder her hands are shaking.

"I'm not buying you any cigarettes."

She puts her hands beneath her legs on the seat to still the shaking. "Some friend you are."

Nothing quite so cruel as principle.

Charlene can't get warm, her body in deep cold, trembling. Even after we've arrived home, even after she's had her cigarette, she still trembles.

I tell her she should eat something, but she says she can't. Not yet. "I'll eat before bedtime," she promises. She asks me to call her brother to bring Nibaa. While we wait, she sits on her recliner, leaning against her electric heating pad, still shivering.

"Do you want a blanket?"

She shakes her head. "No."

Nibaa arrives, cold-pawed and panting and full of excitement, and jumps onto her lap. She winces at the jolt to her legs but doesn't protest. Nibaa sprawls across her chest, belly up. Charlene runs her fingers gently down the dog's belly. "Nibaa'll warm me up."

I drive home to collect my things and come back to spend the night.

The next morning, Charlene looks a thousand times better. Her body has stopped trembling, and her eyes are bright.

"Will you stay until I take my shower?" she asks.

"Do you want me to help you with it?"

"No. I don't think so. If you'll just stay here." She pauses. "Do you think that means I won't be able to take care of myself, since I'm scared to be alone for my shower?"

"No. You'll do fine, Char. You're allowed to be a little scared your first day back."

She takes off her pale blue bathrobe and hangs it over the back of a kitchen chair. Sits down at the table—naked except her underwear—to cover her catheter dressing with plastic baggies. Her small belly heaves with the effort of the correct steps in the correct order.

I cut a baggie in half. She measures out a piece of tape and holds it out. I snip it.

Her skin, the color of sand along a beach or a pale brown sapling, hangs from her tiny frame. She stretches out her arm, and I tape the plastic bag over the dressing on the top right corner of her chest. My fingers slide across her skin, gentle, as I tape. At my touch, her chest heaves violently.

She is naked, helpless, and exposed. Before Charlene, I never realized how helpless the elderly are—how alone their bodies, how trembling their emotions.

But Charlene, sitting naked at the table, holds her chin up, unashamed.

She puts her arm down. The skin of her shoulder bags and wrinkles, and the tape ripples with it. I look at the thin skin of her neck and imagine how the tape will hurt when it is pulled off, the thin skin stretching.

"Mom and Dad still want to come visit you. They're going to come later this morning, after chores."

She shakes her head. "I don't understand why." But I see she holds the honor of it close, her eyes bright with anticipation.

I leave before they come—after Charlene's successful shower, after we fry eggs and bacon and offer even Nibaa a piece. Love permeates the air of the tiny house, as thick and greasy as the bacon smoke.

I escape the emotion-charged atmosphere with relief, slipping out the door into common air with a glow in my belly, as if I've just left revival meetings. Leaving town, I pass Dad and Mom driving in, my brother Benny and sister Elizabeth in the back seat.

"How was the visit?" I ask Charlene later that evening.

Her eyes shine and she smiles. I see something in her face I haven't seen there before. Joy? Lightheartedness? Freedom?

Peace. That's the closest word I can name.

"Your dad helped me understand the answers to a lot of my questions," she says. "They even sang a little song for me. I don't need to blame God anymore."

The information is helpful, but not comprehensive. I piece together the visit as best I can by quizzing Mom later.

Charlene sat in her recliner, while Mom, Dad, Ben, and Liz crowded into the living room, fresh as flowers. Nibaa wiggled, sniffing knees and hands.

They sat. Mom on the rocker, Dad on a kitchen chair beside her, Liz across the room on the wicker chair, and Ben on the footstool, pulled to the side.

"I can see you like owls," Dad said, noticing the owl figurines, the owl pillow, and the round marble-topped table with owls as its stand.

"Yes." Charlene gestured toward the pair of feathery owls sitting on a wooden log on a shelf. "My sister Mary bought those for me at a garage sale. She said she got me a pair of hooters, since I don't have any of my own."

"They didn't say anything to that," she tells me later. "I don't know what they thought of it."

"Why?" I ask. "What are hooters?"

"That's slang for breasts."

I grin. "Mom and Dad don't know that. They would have just thought you were talking about owls."

During the visit, Charlene asked Dad, "How is it fair for God to treat me like this? He gives me so much pain, my life is unlivable."

"There's a verse that says God's ways are higher than our ways," Dad told her. "What's that verse, honey?"

"As the heavens are higher than the earth, so are my ways higher than your ways, and my thoughts than your thoughts," Mom said. "It's in Isaiah ... or is it Psalms?"

They paged through the Bible, found the verse, and read it to her.

"You can still have a purpose for living," Dad told her. "My dad used to sit in his chair most of the time—he had gout and a bad heart and couldn't do much—but he prayed. You can always pray. Maybe God is keeping you on this earth for that very purpose, because someone needs your prayers."

"I'm afraid of dying alone."

"It's natural to fear death," Dad said. "We all do, to a certain extent. But when you understand Jesus, when you know that he loves you and that his purpose in coming to earth was to take the punishment for your sins, and when you trust in him, you don't need to fear death anymore. 'Though I walk through the valley of the shadow of death, I will fear no evil, for thou art with me.'"

Mom paged through Charlene's Bible and found Psalm twenty-three. Dad read all six verses aloud. And then my family members sang to her from the old black *Christian Hymnal* they brought from home.

"When my life work is ended and I cross the swelling tide,
When the bright and glorious morning I shall see;
I shall know my Redeemer when I reach the other side,
And His smile will be the first to welcome me.

I shall know Him, I shall know Him
And redeemed by his side I shall stand,
I shall know Him, I shall know Him
By the prints of the nails in His hand."

A few Sundays later, Charlene asks me, "What good is the Bible to me?"

"Well, the Bible is the basis of everything we believe. Without it, what's the point of being a Christian? You have no basis to believe in Jesus without the Bible."

But slow of ear and thick of brain, I've misheard her question. Charlene didn't ask, *What good is the Bible?* but *What good is the Bible to me?* I don't realize my mistake until I get up to leave.

"I feel lost," she says, her head down, voice disappearing into her lap.

"Is there anything in particular that's making you feel that way?"

She lifts her head. "Yes, there is. I don't know if I should read the Bible or go to church. What good do they do me when I can't understand what I hear or what I read?"

Thus is born our Bible study.

I pick Charlene up every other Monday morning and take her to my house where we sit at the table with Dad and Mom and any siblings that happen along. Charlene wants to study the book of Revelation. This from the woman who told me emphatically, the first time she read it, "I don't like Revelation. It doesn't make any sense." Whether or not she likes Revelation, she's read it four times in her quest to understand it, and now she wants to study this book with my parents.

Revelation, despite its mystical qualities, proves to be a jumpstart for many Bible-paging, concordance-using, life-influencing discussions.

"Let's take turns reading," Dad suggests at our first meeting, his voice friendly and conversational. "How about you go first, Charlene?"

I am grateful for his kindness to guests, when I know him as a private man and a busy farmer. When I was young, he grumbled over too many phone calls and social gatherings. He simply wanted to do his farm chores, and then come in and relax. But now he is taking time—for my sake, for Charlene's sake—to sit down and have a Bible study.

Mom smiles at Charlene, smile wrinkles raying out from her eyes.

Charlene reads the first verse. "Who wrote this, anyway?"

An easy question. I look at Dad, expecting him to tell her it was the apostle John, but he doesn't.

"Let's look it up," he says instead. "I'll get the Bible dictionary from the study."

Of course. Dad won't trivialize her question. He'll look it up, discuss it, and explain. I admire many things about him, but perhaps most of all, I admire his knack for putting people at ease.

The conversation broadens and we move from discussing the author of Revelation to discussing the authors of the other books of the Bible, why the Bible is valid, and why there are so many differences between Christians. Then we talk about swearing, Dad working the topic smoothly into the conversation. I've told him Charlene's tendencies.

"My dad swore constantly when we were kids," she says. "My mom used to say, 'Don't swear. Try a prayer.' But those swear words are in my head so deep, it's hard not to say them."

"I think God understands that," Dad says, "and he also understands if we are making an honest effort. If you mess up, you only have to ask his forgiveness."

She lets out a hoot. "Oh, yeah, I have to ask his forgiveness many times."

We don't make it past the first two verses of Revelation during our first Bible study.

After an hour of discussion, Mom brings out plates, spaghetti, and applesauce cake. A couple of my brothers rush in the door, home from work for their lunch break. They load their plates and sit down at the table, smiling and greeting Charlene before they get busy with eating.

Someone brings up Alzheimer's and how brain activity is supposed to prevent it.

"I guess Char won't have any trouble with Alzheimer's," I say. "She thinks all the time."

"Sometimes I wonder if I'm getting holes in my brain," Charlene says. "I can't remember anything anymore."

"I go out to the shed," Dad says, "and forget what I went out there for. Sometimes I have to come back to the house, to where I started out, to remember."

"And I've already jumped in the van and been on my way to the store," Mom adds, "and couldn't remember what I was going for."

I love this about my parents, their kindness, their warmth and commonness.

Charlene told me once that her dad treated her mom like a doormat, that the girls in their home were expected to remain silent while he discussed the day's work with the boys and had to wait for their food until the boys were served.

In America? I find that hard to imagine.

I look at Mom, her face tipped toward Charlene, smiling and nodding. And Dad. Funny that I still view him as larger than life when other people would maybe just see a small man—a farmer on an outdated farm, pastor of a forgotten Mennonite church—with a balding head and graying hair, eating his spaghetti.

Charlene tells me one day, "You look up at the clouds, and you see how they travel across the sky. No one can stop the clouds. You look down at the river, and you see how it travels across the land. No one can stop the river."

As surely as the clouds and river, our friendship also progresses. Coming to a place of acceptance, we no longer discuss what we are to each other. We are friends, and that is enough.

More and more, I think she likes me. Not just that she needs me or is obsessed with me—a place any rock or Teddy bear could fill—but that she likes me for who I am as a person. I catch myself chattering once, excited and exuberant and senseless, because I am young and the air braces me and possibility lies ahead. But knowing how annoying a chatterbox can be, I apologize.

Charlene smiles. "It's good to have someone here to fill the quiet."

"I talk too fast." I've always hated this about myself.

"Yes," she says. By the look in her eyes, I feel quite suddenly as though my voice, instead of being an annoyance, is beautiful and unique.

And even though I habitually leave behind my scarf or purse or gloves, a haphazardness foreign to Charlene's ordered world, she doesn't seem to mind. Each time I dart back from the car to retrieve something, she smiles as though I have done something precious, the way a fond grandmamma would smile at her granddaughter for mispronouncing a word.

While Charlene calls me her "best friend," I do not return the favor. I tell myself that she might have few friends, but I have many. I refuse to single out an old lady as the best of them.

"No one will miss me when I'm gone," she tells me more than once. "When I die, no one's going to come to my funeral."

At first, I believe her and feel a pitying sort of "serves you right." She should be nice to people while she has the chance. Instead, she is a sharp-tongued, ornery old lady who bosses and manipulates and tells other people exactly what she thinks. So what if she gives money to family members who ask for it? She's only trying to buy their love. And money can't buy friendship.

But as I get to know Charlene better and observe the complexities of her relationships, I change my thinking. She may not have many close friends, but she does have friends. She is far from being despised. Although she's impatient and often unkind, she is also wise, generous, and loyal beyond measure. A woman who commands respect.

Charlene knows things. Somehow. Above doctors, religions, or science books, she trusts her instincts, her observations, and the simplicity of her own thoughts.

We argue about the moon once—an orange moon in autumn.

"Now what would make the moon orange?" she asks.

I don't know and have never thought much about it. If I had, I would have concluded the moon is orange because that's what it is, for mysterious reasons known only to God and the scientists.

The next day, she's figured out the reason. "It's because in the fall, the farmers are busy harvesting, and they stir up dust. And it's all that dust floating around in the air that makes the moon look orange."

"How do you know that?" I ask.

"I thought about it."

"I don't think that could be the reason. I'll go home and look it up."

"Suit yourself."

I research orange moons online and discover the color does indeed come from dust, smoke, or pollution in the air. The tiny particles refract light rays, causing the moon to appear orange.

I would never have been smart enough to figure that out. I depend on books for my answers. If the book is wrong, I am wrong.

I try to describe her peculiar quality to her one day—her intuitive powers, her refusal to think within someone else's framework, the quality in her that commands respect.

"You have ... something. I don't know what to call it."

Charlene watches me, face still, with that manner she has of absorbing every word.

And then, triumphantly, I find it. "You have *ability*."

She says nothing, but her eyes absorb the tribute, satisfied.

PART FOUR—NEW BIRTH

I cradled it in my two hands
fingers light
against its throbbing
careful
not to bruise it.

DECEMBER 2012

A deranged man takes a gun—like a sane man takes a lawn mower—and mows down a roomful of schoolchildren. The government discusses jail or the death penalty.

"They should strip him naked," Charlene says as I'm driving her home from Bible study one day, "and make him run across that field and back." She motions to the field, covered in a foot of snow. I imagine Wisconsin's winter winds striking a naked body, bare feet breaking the icy crust, legs plunging deep. "If he survived, he could live. If he died, too bad. That's what the Native Americans did."

A few days later, we attend the funeral of Mary's ex-husband, the father of Sondra and Adam. Charlene comes straight from dialysis, asking her driver to drop her off at the funeral home. She's asked me to take her to the burial afterward. I arrive late and slip in the back, but after the service, I find her near the front sitting beside her sister from the rez.

I know she must feel sick from dialysis, but her tiny, wrinkled face shows little distress and almost appears to be smiling. Charlene says nothing when she sees me, but her sister says, "She's not feeling good. She wants to go right home."

So I drive my car around back and walk Charlene, who is unusually docile and quiet, outside. We meet Mary, who's come outside for a cigarette. She hugs Charlene, tells her she understands, and thanks her for coming.

"They played 'Taps,'" Charlene tells me back at her place. "When I heard them play 'Taps,' I knew I couldn't go to the burial. To me, 'Taps' is the saddest sound in the world."

I think back through all the deaths she and I have experienced between us during the last year. Her nephew. Max. Mary's ex-husband. My grandpa, my uncle, my cousin, the boy in the logging accident. You can't count death. There is no reckoning of it.

Death is wrong.

I don't understand it and refuse to think about it. None of those deaths affect me, anyway, I tell myself. The whole world could die around me, and I'll only get a slightly numb, surprised sort of feeling, because it's not me and it's not the people close to me who've died. Even Grandpa Miller, who lived ten hours away in Indiana, was distant.

I wonder what I'll do when Charlene dies. I think of that a lot. How will it hurt and in what parts of me and will I be able to deal with it? When winter is so cold, and so many people die, and dialysis hurts so bad, I pray she can go. Or think of praying that. I can't bring myself to actually do it.

At Charlene's last heart checkup, the cardiologist was surprised to see her looking so well. "Judging from your last appointment with me, I expected you to be in far worse shape by now."

"It's because of you that I'm doing so well," Charlene told me later. "I live just to see you."

"You're a tough old broad, aren't you?" the cardiologist had said, her voice full of admiration and affection.

A tough old broad. It's not how I would describe her.

"Did you ever like to go hunting, Char?" I asked once.

She was tipped back in her recliner, oxygen tubing in her nose, the hum of the machine beside her.

"When I had surgery for my heart, I was cut open from here to here." With the tips of her fingers, she slashed from chest to underarm. "When my brother Emmet and his wife came to visit, Emmet stepped into the room and when he saw me, he was like this ..." Charlene traced tears down her cheeks. "He turned around and walked out. His wife went out and got him and brought him back in.

"'Sister,' Emmet told me, 'when you recover from this, whatever you want, I'll help you get it.'

"So after I was better, I told him I wanted to go hunting. It was the only time I went. I saw a beautiful buck, but I couldn't shoot it. I couldn't bring myself to kill such an animal."

"You mean you had the chance to shoot one and you didn't?"

She nodded, smiling. "She's not as tough as she pretends to be."

A tough old broad. I also said it to her once before I realized my mistake. During the autumn now past, with trees bare branched and winter drifting in, I told her, "You're the toughest person I've ever met."

"Really?"

I nodded. "You're different than anyone else I know. You're tough."

But later, as I lay on crinkly dead leaves under trees in the yard, felt the wind rise with the approaching storm, an acrid smell of corn silage drifting from the piles in the field, I mulled over the conversation and realized I'd gotten it exactly wrong.

Charlene is not the toughest person I ever met. She's the most fragile. The flesh beneath her tiled plates is delicate, rose petal baby flesh—pinchable, touchable, soft.

Funny what a shell can hide.

She sits small and silent and in pain. Her worst time, after dialysis. I sit in the rocker, she in the recliner, her body stiff.

"Sometimes when the pain is so bad, all I want to do is lie down in bed and die, but I don't do it for fear I will actually die. The only way I can get through when it's like that is to think of Jesus and what he suffered. You have no idea what it is."

"I know. I have no idea what all you suffer."

"I don't understand why God would do this to me."

"It's not God who does it to you. It's this messed-up old world. God gives you a way out of it. All of this will seem like absolutely nothing the moment you step into heaven."

"So until then I just have to suffer?"

I hesitate, trying to think of a way to fine tune my answer, to make it bearable.

"I just have to suffer."

"Yeah," I concede.

We are silent for a time, Nibaa wiggling and snuffling at my knee. I stroke her ears, and she quiets, sits with ears perked and furry face uplifted, absorbing my touch.

"Now I have a question for you," I say. "It's one you probably don't know the answer to. I don't know the answer."

Her face perks like Nibaa's.

"If you hadn't had health problems and pain all your life, would you have sought after God? Would you still have learned to depend on Jesus?"

"I don't know."

"Only God knows that." I pick up Nibaa's ragged red horse and toss it across the room. She races after it, wildly excited.

"I might still be hell on wheels."

"You might. Some people go to their death beds that way, hardened."

She nods and winces, her legs and back stiffening.

We are still until the spasm passes, Nibaa wild against my knee with her toy.

Charlene stoops to take off her socks and shoes, and I move to the floor to help her. I pull the long knee socks off as gently as I can, place them into her shoes, and set the shoes beneath the end table. "Do you think massaging your legs would help?"

"If I could stand to have them touched."

I touch her legs below her rolled up jeans lightly. "Does this hurt?"

"No."

"And this, and this?" I keep rubbing, but you could scarcely call it a massage as my fingers don't press the muscle at all, only brush it.

"No, it doesn't hurt."

Her legs are like two stuffed sausages ready to burst their casings—dark near the ankles, bruised in several places, smooth and hairless.

"I've never had to worry about shaving," she says. "I never had hair on my legs or under my arms."

"Really?"

"And yes," she says, grinning, "I do have pubic hair."

I grin back. Who but Charlene would say this? Flustered, I rub a little harder in one spot.

"That's enough now," she says.

Janis is a small woman, with skinny elbows, a square face, and beautifully groomed hair the color of gray goose feathers. Not for Janis the faded uniforms and scruffy tennis shoes some of the other CNA's wear. She comes to the nursing home dressed for her work as an aide in bright scrubs and small, neat shoes.

I am deathly afraid of her.

I didn't start out that way. At first, we were friends. Janis was friendly and competent, and she loved a good gossip. Shy at my new job with these casual, confident non-Mennonites, I was all admiration and interest. Janis asked me questions about the Mennonites, and we had a discussion about denominational differences, standing over a bed.

I suppose the problem started with a small mistake, a misunderstood phrase, or a hectic shift. I might have gotten sidetracked by a call light and failed to communicate with Janis where I was, or maybe I was too slow at caring for a resident, or maybe, as happens in my sometimes-scatterbrained way, I forgot a task I should have done.

No matter the cause, Janis yelled at me. At least, that is what I called her sharp words, impatient tone of voice, and look of contempt.

She brought a bag of Butterfingers to work the next day—she knew that I liked them—and we tried to make up.

But I am nervous with her now, self-conscious and clumsy.

There are other episodes, with Janis impatient and snappy. Each time, I grow more intimidated and more resentful. Any further attempts at friendship are only contrived.

I contain a weak, milky substance in my body that must be at peace with all people at all times. I've always gotten along with everyone before this, have worked hard to do so. Now, because Janis does not like me, a heaviness comes over me, a hurting in my stomach. When she yells, I cannot yell back. I can only go into a closet and cry, as reduced in dignity and great in hurt as a five-year-old.

I blame my spinelessness on my parents. If they had yelled at me when I was young—if they had been a little mean, ever—I might have become hardened and immune or developed nails to defend myself. But they didn't, and I haven't.

I stop at Charlene's on my supper break one evening, crying after yet another episode with Janis. I wish I could hide my weakness from Charlene's sharp eyes, but I cannot stop the tears.

"What's wrong, Luci?"

"Nothing."

She waits.

"It's just I ... Janis ..." I heave words between sobs. "... she yells at me, and it makes me cry."

"Come here, Luci." Charlene hugs me, and I cry against her shoulder. "How could anyone be cruel to such a sweet little girl as you?"

"I'm not always sweet."

"I've never known you to be any different."

I don't tell Charlene that Janis reminds me of her. Janis is easily critical. Just like Charlene. She is competent, smart, opinionated, afraid of no one. Just like Charlene. When something goes wrong, she lets me know it is my fault. Just like Charlene. But with Janis, there is not the need of a lonely old lady to bridge the gap.

I grow clumsy around Janis, making awkward mistakes. I grow tense and nervous and too eager to please. And just like Charlene, Janis will yell at me—I call it yelling, though it is only a tone of voice, an emphatic tilt of the chin—then make up for it in friendliness the rest of the shift.

I cry in the utility room once, next to the garbage cans and laundry bins. Janis finds me there, and we talk. She comforts me in a voice as soothing and melodic as water and gives me a hug. "We should have had this talk a long time ago."

"We'll be friends," I say with a burst of affection.

But we aren't.

We cannot be because we are not equal. I greatly admire her—I gravitate toward the opinionated and the self-assured—and hold out my heart hopefully. We seem almost friends.

But again, Janis gets impatient and yells at me.

I hate her then and wish she would go to hell. I imagine her there, burning. Frightened at what is in me, I forgive her on the sweet summer lawn in front of the nursing home during the fifteen minutes of my break. I won't try to be friends with her anymore except on the surface, where it doesn't matter anyway.

But I mention Janis frequently to Charlene, now that I've discovered she is sympathetic instead of scornful. "I have to work with Janis tonight," I'll say. "Pray it goes good."

And she will nod gravely. "I always pray for you."

On a blustery day in January, I stop at Charlene's on my supper break. These visits have become like clockwork now.

"Hi, Char!" I swing inside, smiling and vibrant. Charlene, pained and stiff on her recliner, smiles when she sees me. I clip the leash on Nibaa and stand at the door while she runs into the yard to do her business. When she's finished, I let her into her crate so her feet will dry out and poke a piece of dog biscuit through the grate.

"Should I fix your taco?"

Charlene nods, and I take the taco meat from the refrigerator along with the plastic container of shredded lettuce and another of cheese. Nowadays, instead of Taco John's after every dialysis trip, she asks her driver to go through the Taco John's drive-thru on Monday, when she orders enough taco fixings to last the week.

I take two hard-shelled tacos from the box in the cupboard, break the top off one of them, spread it with seasoned meat and a little cheese, lay the top in place again, wrap it in paper towel, and warm it in the microwave for fifteen seconds. Charlene likes things done just so.

I carry the warmed taco to Charlene in the living room, along with a knife and container of sour cream, and return to the kitchen to prepare her second taco, for later.

I remember to let Nibaa out of her crate. "Did Nibaa have supper?"

"I don't know. Check."

There's still dog food in the tin can beside the sink, which means Nibaa hasn't been fed yet. When Charlene feeds her in the mornings, she always fills that tin can and sets it beside the sink, so she won't forget in the evening.

I feed Nibaa and help myself to some ice cream from the freezer. I hate packing lunches, but Charlene never seems to mind if I help myself to ice cream or a taco or a peanut butter and jelly sandwich at her place.

I go into the living room and sit on the rocking chair with my bowl of ice cream. The *Andy Griffith Show* is on and I watch until the commercials. "How was dialysis?"

She shrugs. "Okay."

"It's a good thing I'm not working with Janis today," I say. "She didn't look very happy when I saw her ... at least not toward me."

Charlene tilts her face toward me, cheeks high-planed, chin like a bone. "Luci, when are you going to just get over it? Janis doesn't have to look happy. She doesn't have to be all smiley face every time she walks past you. 'Oh, there comes Luci, gotta put on my happy face.' If she doesn't feel like smiling, she won't smile. She's not out to get Luci."

I feel my cheeks heat and withdraw, stone-hearted, into a private, seething world.

I work with Janis the next evening and don't feel scared of her one bit. I am still too busy being mad at Charlene.

If she had been wrong—and if she had been kinder—she would have been easier to forgive. But much as it pains me to admit it, I know she is right.

There is no sin so hard to forgive as the sin of being right.

"I think your yelling at me helped me," I tell Charlene the following morning, grinding humility from my gut like cookie dough. Only because I know Jesus wants us to be humble, and for no other reason than that. "I really did think Janis was out to get me."

She smiles, pleased and forgiving and gracious. "Just like your dad said in his sermon the other Sunday, I can open the gates, but you have to make your own choices. I want to show you the way, Luci."

I smile, half amused and half pretending. Old people are foolish this way, seeing themselves as founts of wisdom for young people to follow.

But by Monday morning—after a fun Sunday off with my friends—my resentment toward Charlene is gone. I lie in bed in the early morning, awakened by the reflected snow light coming bright through my window. That's just what I needed, I think. Some interaction, something different to think about. Charlene doesn't have that. For her, it's the same day after day after day.

I feel a burst of sympathy and understanding.

No wonder she gets crabby.

I grab my cell phone from the nightstand and hit the number three—the speed dial for Charlene. Today is Bible study day, and I promised to come early so we can make some stops beforehand.

"Hello." Her voice holds the quiet crackle of morning.

"Would it be okay if I come at nine thirty?"

"Yeah, that would be fine."

"Will that be enough time?"

A pause, as though she's unsure. "I guess so."

"What all stops do you need to make?"

Suddenly, her voice turns vile with rage. "Give me time to think, will you?"

"I wasn't trying to hurry you."

"Yes, you were."

"No, I wasn't, Char. I just asked a question."

I arrive at her place at nine thirty-five, sweep off her porch, and let out Nibaa.

Charlene says—and I can tell she's trying to order her words just right—"Could you turn off the humidifier and then push the pump all the way in, down to the bottom? I couldn't get it down all the way."

We have a notoriously hard time communicating over tasks. Often, I fail to grasp her carefully iterated instructions. Often, she grows impatient, not understanding how I can misunderstand what she has phrased so precisely.

I squat beside the humidifier on the kitchen floor and turn the knob to Off. Then, I try to figure out what Charlene means by the pump at the bottom. Does she mean underneath the humidifier? Inside it? I see that the white insert isn't sitting as snugly as it should and jiggle it. "Did you mean this?"

I hate to ask. I dread her response.

"No," she says, and her voice vibrates impatience. She marches across the kitchen with longsuffering steps and lifts the white insert, pointing at the pump inside. *See?* her actions say. *I have to show you since you're too dumb to understand.*

And that is the point when my goose is cooked.

My turkey fried.

My kidney stoned.

All of a sudden, I am tired of Charlene's impatience, her temper, her attitude.

I am tired of Charlene.

I don't like her in the store when she drops her package of roast chuck and swears. I don't like her at the checkout counter when I fail to understand her injunction to remove the center ads from her *Ladysmith News*, and she grabs the paper from my hands and removes them herself. I don't like her on the way to Bible study when she complains in her crow voice about the cost of the nutritional drink she uses.

"I might as well get beer. It'd be cheaper, and it has just as many calories."

I don't answer. She's probably just trying to get a rise out of me.

"What do you think, Luci?"

Go ahead. I don't care, is what I think. Drinking beer might not be such a bad idea. I cared for a lady at the nursing home once who refused to eat but drank a beer every day. For weeks, it must have been the only thing keeping her alive.

But I refuse to give Charlene such approbation.

Typical for me, I circumvent the question. "What is beer made of?"

"Beer is made with hops."

"I don't know what that is."

"Oats." Again, I hear the impatience in her voice.

"Oats." I think it over with exaggerated intent. "Well, that's a grain. But I don't know if beer has any nutrients or not."

When we get to my place, I sit a couple chairs down from Charlene at the table. I can't stand to be too close. I try to do this unobtrusively. I don't want Mom and Dad to notice my pettiness. But I want Charlene to notice. I try not to look at her when she talks to me.

"Luci, where's the key to my oxygen tank?"

Charlene carries a portable oxygen tank with her whenever she's away from home for more than a couple of hours. Otherwise, she soon finds it difficult to breathe. But without the key to open the valve, the oxygen tank will not work.

"The key was right here when I got out the tank." I point to the side of the tank where the key should have hung and wait for Charlene's annoyance, her snapping words.

But she's thought this one through and has determined to be patient. "Do you think you might have laid it on the bookshelf at home?" she asks, her voice friendly.

"No. But it might be out on the back seat of the car." I remember how I dropped the oxygen tank on the seat, haphazardly, when we left her house. I go out to the car, praying to find the key, and see it immediately on the floor in front of the back seat. I snatch it up thankfully and take it inside.

I don't say anything, just kneel beside the oxygen tank with the key in my hand.

"Didn't find it?" Charlene asks in her friendliest voice. "It's probably at home on the bookshelf."

I've already fit the key over the valve.

"I think she has it there," Dad says.

I try to turn the key, but it won't budge.

"The other way," Charlene snaps, in her *you're an idiot* voice. "Lefty loosey."

Turning the key, I brood over her treatment of me in front of my family. They, who value courtesy and kindness, must wonder why I am enamored with such a cranky old lady. They can't know about the good times, about how nice she can be when we're alone. In front of my family, I feel like a humiliated wife, hiding the bruises.

I nurse the anger in my head, enjoying it.

God will get you for this, I remind myself. *God will get you.* But I don't care.

Driving back to Charlene's house after Bible study, I turn on my contemporary Christian music. For me, with my tradition of Mennonite acapella, contemporary Christian is the equivalent of hard rock. Or, at least, the closest I can come with the materials on hand. I listen to my music and tune Charlene out completely, letting the scowl between my eyebrows show, not caring if I annoy her with my music.

She beats her foot in time, showing her appreciation. Silly me. And to think I've only played soft hymns and old-time gospel music all this time with her. I am used to Mennonite old ladies and forgot that Charlene was of the Elvis generation and would like something with a beat.

Just inside the door, as I turn to go, she looks at me and smiles sweetly. "Thank you for all you do for me. Thank you for your friendship and tenderness and love."

Tears spring into my eyes.

"Are you sad, Luci?"

"Not exactly. I'm just upset."

"What's wrong?"

I look away.

She seats herself at the table, waiting. After a while, she says, "I'm your friend, right? Just tell me about it. Don't let it fester."

Her voice is reasonable, calm. And she waits. No person on earth can wait like Charlene can. She waits with openness, but no curiosity. So enticing.

I look at my feet, wondering if the words will come. They must come. She is right. I don't have to let this fester. And she is listening, her face open.

I gather courage. *Make the words simple and direct*, I tell myself.

"I'm just angry and upset."

"Why? I tried to watch my p's and q's."

"I know ... no, I didn't know." I hesitate longer, gather the words from my pocket. "I just don't like the way you talk to me sometimes."

Her face changes in an instant, growing skeptical and angry.

"I feel like you treat me like used furniture."

I say it quietly, hurriedly, but it is the thing I meant to say in the first place. I always do it this way, say last the thing I mean as first.

Her face hardens, a veil of skepticism dropping over her eyes. "For whatever it was that was done or said, I apologize. It won't happen again."

I look at her, clearheaded now that my accusation is made. The worst—the confrontation—is over, and I can look her in the face. *She doesn't really mean that. She doesn't even know why I feel this way, and she's not asking.*

I wonder if I should sit down across from her and try to explain, try to understand. But she's turned away.

I put on my boots. "Bye."

On the way home, I pull over in a field lane on the gravel road that leads to my house and tell God I am not at all repentant for my anger and unforgiving attitude. I tell him I know it's wrong, but I don't care. "But please, God, because you are so kind and so good, please help me anyway. Help me to get straightened out and want to have the right attitudes again. Because I just don't feel happy, and I want to feel happy again. Please take care of this whole mess because I'm not capable of even trying."

"Are you tired?" Mom asks when I get home. "You look tired."

"Maybe a little." I pluck a blueberry muffin from the basket in the kitchen and sit on the couch to eat it, not looking at Mom, willing myself not to cry. I will pretend to be normal, just tired. I lie on the couch and pull a blanket over me and go to sleep that way, drifting in and out.

When I wake, I have peace. It stole across me while I slept, drifting in like feathers when I wasn't awake to prevent it with thoughts. God does this sometimes, lays peace over me while I sleep, tucking me in like a child beneath down. I inevitably chase the peace away, watch the fleeting wisps of it disappear while I worry about how to hold on to it.

But you can't hold on to peace.

It is a gift.

The following day, when I stop by on my lunch break, Charlene is exaggeratedly sweet, talking in long, formal sentences, using "pleases" and "dears" with abandon.

Maybe I should be angry, but I'm not. I remember how she said the day before, "It won't happen again," and I believe her. It's all I asked. I really don't care how else Charlene acts, as long as she doesn't yell. It's the yelling that hurts.

So I take her exaggerated sweetness in good faith, and when I leave fifteen minutes later, peace reigns between us.

The following day when I go to see her, she's grown gentle, in that deep way only the vehement can be. Her words are quiet, haloed by love.

"Thank you for the way you treat me," I tell her when I say goodbye. "I love coming over to see you because you treat me like royalty and where else am I going to get that?"

Charlene smiles, proud.

Charlene smokes half a cigarette—all she will allow herself at one time now—and snuffs it out in the green glass ashtray. Sitting across from her, I move my face away from the smoke, look out the window at the snowy yard and a lady in a purple coat walking on the sidewalk two blocks down.

We've been talking about morals.

"Nobody has them anymore," Charlene says. "Young people have sex when they want to, and then, if they want to, they go ahead and have a kid without being married."

I understand. "It makes you feel helpless, doesn't it?"

She nods. The purple-coated lady has disappeared. "I wonder what good reading this Book is going to do me." She motions toward her Bible lying beside the ashtray, her voice bitter. "Who's going to care if I end up in heaven or hell? I can't think of one person who cares."

"I care."

"Why?"

"Because I love you so much." My eyes slide to hers and away, uneasy because the words sound stiff and artificial, as though I've cut them from a manual and pasted them to my lips. Charlene needs my words to be genuine. "Besides, even if I didn't love you, I would still care."

I think of Janis. I would want to see even Janis in heaven. I think about telling Charlene that but abandon the thought.

"Why?"

"Because ..." I think of all the people in the world, all the people I care about and don't know how to help. How to guarantee heaven for a mob of sinners when most of them don't seem to care? Tears come to the back of my eyes. "I just wish there was more I could do to help people."

"But what does that have to do with me?"

"You. I love you. I want to go to heaven, and I want you to go there too. I would have no greater joy than that."

Her wrinkles relax, and her eyes brighten, satisfied. "What do you think we'll do when we get there?"

"I don't know." I think about it for a few moments. "You like the outdoors and I do too … the beauty of it. And heaven must be so much more beautiful than anything we've seen. I think we'll enjoy its beauty, walk beside the river together."

"Yesterday, on the way to dialysis, every tree, every twig between here and Barron was frosted in snow. Heaven can't be any more beautiful than that."

"Oh, I bet it could."

She shakes her head. "Heaven can't be any more beautiful than that, and that shows me heaven is what you make of it."

I smile, looking out the window. "But think of the sky. Would you ever have guessed there could be so many different colors of blue?"

She nods. "I've thought about that too."

"I think in heaven we'll see new colors we can't see here. And we'll hear new sounds."

She tilts her head. "So in heaven, I know you'll be looking for colors."

I nod.

"And I'll be taking care of all the baby animals." She speaks in a tone so simple and sweet—like a child's—I want to cry. "When I see those little animals on TV, I just love them. That's all I want to do—take care of them. But in heaven, I might need you to help me with the baby elephant."

I laugh a free rolling laugh, and she looks pleased.

"I love God so much, Luci. I love him with all my heart and soul and mind. And when I see a thunderstorm, I'm not afraid. Once, lightning passed right over my head. It came in through one window and went out the window behind me. But I'm not afraid of the storms. They make me think of God's power. I like to think he's just playing tricks. Like he's saying, 'I'll scare the bejeebers out of her.' But maybe I'm a warped old lady."

I laugh again. "No, you're not."

"You have to be a little warped to live in this world," she says. "There was a Mexican foreman back when I worked at the factory—a fat Mexican foreman. Well, he became a born-again Christian, and one by one he called each of the employees into his office and talked to them about Jesus. Not necessarily about the Bible, but about Jesus. There was one girl—she was well-liked—he called her into his office, and they were in there the whole shift, talking. That's eight hours of talking, Luci! A week or two later, they told us they were going to get married. She was a pretty girl and the daughter of a wealthy man. She could have had anyone she wanted. But he had her convinced they would go to heaven together. I don't think anyone can promise heaven to another human being."

It's funny how Charlene's stories have a way of opening my mind as nothing else can. For the first time, I understand her under-the-surface, never-quite-expressed antagonism against the "born again" people.

I've always viewed "born again" as a miracle of new beginnings, a gift from God. Charlene, maybe, views "born again" as just someone's bragging rights, a way for some self-righteous individual—a fat, lazy foreman, maybe—to say to another, "I've had an experience with God, and you haven't. I'm right with him and you're not. If you want to have good standing with God, be like me."

"Are they really born again?" she asked Dad at a recent Bible study.

Then, too, I saw as she must see. So many of them— these born-again Christians—so vocal in their correctness and in their right standing before God. They've prayed a prayer—copied it, maybe, like the continuing reel in an organ grinder's music box—parroted a few words about Jesus Christ being the only way to heaven and suddenly, they are born again and better than their neighbors.

"Are they really?" Charlene asked.

Dad looked at her and shook his head. "I don't know."

As a minister, he's often embroiled against his will in the friction and hurt feelings that come between Christians when one party feels they are following the Bible better than another party. I remember what he told us children once. "People are all looking for God's approval. And people hurt other people when they tell them they're not meeting God's approval, when they hold that over their heads as a weapon."

At a later Bible study, he told Charlene, "Never let anyone make you feel inferior before God. It doesn't matter if you're a baby Christian or if you've followed God for many years, he views you both equally. He hears your prayers just the same. Your relationship with God is your own, and no one can take that from you."

Nibaa pushes against my knee, pants at the door, and I get up to let her out. Nibaa makes quick work of her needs— the snow cold on her feet—and when she's finished, I put her into her crate with a piece of dog biscuit.

"I read a verse the other day," Charlene says when I sit down again. "And it didn't make any sense to me. I won't try to quote it because I can't remember it, but it said how the good works we do for our congregation—I'll say congregation so I don't have to say church or denomination—how they don't save us, but our salvation is a gift from God. That doesn't make sense. If being good doesn't save us, what use is it to be good? And why should anyone try to do good?"

"I know that verse! I don't know where it's found, but it goes something like this: 'By grace are ye saved through faith, and that not of yourselves, it is the gift of God. Not of works, lest any man should boast. For we are his workmanship, created in Christ Jesus unto good works, which God hath before ordained that we should walk in them.'"

She nods. "That's it."

I pray for words. "What you said is exactly right," I tell her. "Our good works don't save us because the Bible says, 'All our righteousness is as filthy rags.' We can't measure up to God's holiness. He doesn't look down and say, 'O look, that person's doing such a good job, I want him for mine.' No. His salvation is a gift. Instead of us doing good works for God, we accept Christ into our lives and then God does good works through us. 'We are his workmanship, created in Christ Jesus unto good works.'"

Her face is clear and open.

"That seems backward, doesn't it?" I say.

"Yes."

"It works though."

She nods, understanding in her face.

"It's so simple," I say, "but it's so hard for people to understand. Maybe it's because we don't understand our own natures. We don't understand we are born in sin."

"What do you mean, born in sin?"

"Born with sinful natures."

"Say it one more time."

I squint at her. "What do you mean?"

"Say it in a different way, so I know what you're talking about."

"I mean we're born with a bent toward sin. Like a baby. They're so innocent, but when they're still tiny they have that self-interested will, that desire to get what they want and to have their own way. It doesn't seem so cute anymore when they reach adulthood."

TURTLE HEART

I am a child, maybe four, lying on the bed sobbing because Dad has spanked me.

"That's enough," he tells me sternly.

But I am heartbroken and cannot stop. I jump when he reaches toward me, and my body grows hot. He lifts me up and spanks me again.

It's not fair, I think. How can I help it if I need to cry? Then, quite suddenly—and my childish mind grasps this with surprise—I *can* stop crying. I realize I could have stopped all along if I had wanted to. And I know, quite clearly, that I have only been feeling sorry for myself, nothing more.

Years later, that is the only spanking I remember, since my parents spanked rarely. Now, I have forgotten the pain of the spanking or the reason I was spanked. But I still remember the surprising realization of that sneaky person inside myself who was a whiner and a wanter and didn't like to be bossed. Remembering, I know that children are far smarter than I give them credit for, that these innocent, round-eyed creatures are aware—as are all humans—of their own wills and desires, and that they struggle for them, hard.

Sometimes, now that I am older and responsible, I long for the easy peace of being four years old, of lying on a bed with my will subdued and knowing I must listen to Dad because he knows best.

There was security in that knowledge—yes—and humility. And in my adult mind trapped by ego, such sincere humility is hard to come by.

FEBRUARY 2013

Orange roses. They are the color of Char's heart. She buys them on Valentine's Day, nine days before her death, and they are delicate and vibrant and generous with their orange.

Just like Char.

When we arrive at my house for Bible study that day, I give her my arm and walk beside her in the jolting of slow, uneven steps through snow. I wait while she uses the doorknob to pull herself up over the door jamb and into the house. Mom meets her in the entranceway as she always does, beaming, warm as fresh-tilled earth.

I return to the car for the roses, swathed in shopping bags to protect them from the cold, and set them on the dining room table.

And then, the revealing. The pulling off of bags. The oohing and ahhing, the sniffing, the gentle touching. Charlene's face looks young, her thousand wrinkles alight and lithesome.

I see her happiest when I see her here, in Dad and Mom's kitchen, with my mom smiling at her and all my siblings laughing at her jokes.

Before we arrive at my house, though, there is the courthouse. We stop there to get Charlene a case of her protein drinks, which she buys at a discount through a community health program.

I seldom visit the courthouse and, unfamiliar with the parking lot, I dawdle with the car in front of the building, looking for a spot close so Charlene won't have far to walk.

"Pull over there and park," she says impatiently, pointing at an empty strip of concrete next to a pile of snow.

I hesitate.

"Right there!" she snaps.

"No!" I make my voice as angry and impatient as I can. "I'm going to drop you off right here, and then I'm going to go and park. And you don't need to get impatient, and that place you suggested isn't even a parking place."

Charlene becomes immediately meek. I jog around the car and help her walk inside. She is small on my arm—tiny—with an air about her of trying to be good. How can one person be so maddening and yet so pleasing?

On the way to my house afterward, with the flowers swathed in plastic on the back seat, I drive a little too fast on the icy road, and the car skids.

Charlene swallows the triumphant "See?" that is rising to her lips. "These slippery roads sure can surprise a person," she says instead.

On the way home after Bible study, I turn on my contemporary Christian music, put my eyes to the road, and tune Charlene out. Quite suddenly, I am tired of her. The hours of time I've spent with her—hours when I could have been writing—pile in my mind like an endless mountain. It's not her fault. She's done nothing to make me feel this way. Today, for the entire day after that first brief episode, she treated me with kindness and great respect.

I pull up in front of her little white house and look over to see her staring at me. "Did I do anything to upset you today, sweetie?"

"No ... well, I was a little upset when you were grumpy to me earlier, but then I was grumpy back, so I didn't need to be upset."

I get out of the car and go around to the passenger's side. Charlene climbs out carefully and slips her hand into the crook of my elbow. "When was I grumpy?"

We step slowly toward the house.

"At the courthouse, when we couldn't find a parking place and you yelled at me. But I yelled back, so then I didn't need to be upset."

"You can always yell at me," she says, "because I always give in right away."

And she is right, I realize. After a lifetime of impatience and broken relationships, Charlene values friendship above all else. She maybe does not always control her tongue and her impatience like she should, but she is humble with her friends, willing to suffer any indignity or slight or blame for the preserving of the relationship.

"Sorry for being grumpy," she says when we reach the house.

"You can be grumpy sometimes if you want," I tell her, repentant. "You're sweet."

She raises her eyebrows as though skeptical of such a description.

But she is. Achingly, piercingly sweet in a way that I, with all my carefully calculated words, my cautions and inhibitions, could never be.

Back home that evening, I check my email and find one from Jake.

Jake!

I've wanted him so badly, for so long, but we haven't seen each other in months. I'd given up on him.

But here—this email—he is asking me to date.

I do not feel happy, only stunned. I am sitting on a couch with an email open in front of me in a strange home and a different world.

Jake!

I must answer him. I form the answer in my mind and type it onto the screen in front of me, making it brief and to the point because I am wildly shy. I don't mess around with the answer all the Mennonite girls I know always give: "I'll think and pray about it." Not for Mennonites a hasty decision on a matter as serious as dating.

Maybe he'll think I'm desperate … but today is Valentine's Day, and on Valentine's Day, you have to say yes right away.

My life is turning out perfectly, like a story in a book.

I call Charlene early the next morning.

"Good morning," she says, her voice warm and lilting.

"Last night I got this email from a guy I know," I say, plunging into my news immediately, "the guy I liked—I mean, I wanted him—forever. And he wants me to date him. It'll be long-distance dating, but that's okay with me."

"I think it's wonderful you can have somebody of your own," she says, warm and gracious. I expected ire. "Then when I walk on to heaven, you'll have somebody to help you through."

I am awed. I've been thinking of Charlene's love as a needy, selfish thing, but I've been wrong. She really does love me better than she loves herself.

Later in the day, when I go to see her on my supper break, her mood has changed. She sits stiff, formal, and cold, talking to me in short, snapped phrases. Strangely, this satisfies me. I want her to be jealous.

"I want you to know it doesn't matter if I have a boyfriend, he will never take your place in my heart," I tell her. "And when the time comes that you should die and walk on to heaven, you will always stay in my heart, until the day I die and come to see you again."

"It's nice of you to say so," she says, smiling stiffly, disbelief in her eyes.

"It's true." I reach into my purse and pull out the printed page I've brought along. "Would you like to read the email he sent me? So you can get a picture of what he's like?"

"No," she says, quickly. Her face winces and closes as though I have slapped it.

And I am glad.

Over the next few days, I barely mention Jake to Charlene. I don't tell her the reason I can't come to see her Sunday morning is that Jake and I have planned a phone call. I'll take it slowly, give her time to adjust so she won't feel pushed out.

I visit her Sunday evening instead. As I fry hamburgers on the stove, their grease hot in the air, I bring up something I've had on my mind ever since I first knew her.

"I want to write a book about you, Charlene. We have such an unusual friendship, you and I, it would make a unique book. I want to write about it."

She contemplates, the folds of skin near her mouth deepening.

"Could I bring my recorder tomorrow morning, and you could tell me stories from your past, and I could write them down? I love hearing your stories."

"Yes. We could do that."

I bring my little Sony recorder the next morning, and she tells me many things. Stories I've heard before and stories that are new.

There is one that sticks in my mind, because I know she thinks it important.

"Last year—and it probably was the wrong thing to do—but last year at the family reunion, I just came in from outside, and I was coming this way, and I met John at the corner."

John, the brother who made her childhood miserable with teasing.

"He said, 'Howdy, Sis, how are you doing?'

"I looked at him right straight in the eye and I said, 'John, you have irritated me all my life. You are a rotten son of a ...'" Charlene drops her voice to a whisper to finish the curse. "He did that to me when we were young, and I had to carry that all that time inside. That was my mean streak. That's what made me so mean."

"Your anger at John?"

She nods. "'Cause anything he could do that he knew would hurt my feelings, he did it. Even to the point that he threw rocks at the barn windows because he had seen me out there washing them. Right after I got done washing them he started breaking them, even though he knew he'd get a whipping. He was just a mean little swine, that's all there is to it! That's the way he grew up. How he got a wife and she stayed with him is beyond me. His children left home early 'cause they didn't like him. Then it finally dawned on him, 'Yeah, maybe I am too mean,' and so he was good to the youngest. She adored him. And his older children both talk to him now that they're older and wiser. They don't hold it against him."

"But you still do, huh?"

"I did. But it doesn't make any difference to me now. I got my two cents in. But it's horrible to confess, even to you, my best friend, that I would say something like that to my brother. See, when I was young, I called him that name, and Mom told me, 'Well, if he's that and you're his sister, what does that make you?' I never, ever called anybody a bad name from that day on until the family reunion. And when I said that to him then I meant it, and he knew I meant it. And he knew there was nothing he could do about it. So I'm at peace with John, even if it took fifty years. Bizarre, eh?"

I am glad that in her own way, in her own time, Charlene has come to forgiveness.

Wednesday, on my supper break, I go to Charlene's house as usual. She sits at the table, playing cards. Nibaa is still in her crate.

"Did Joyce just drop you off from dialysis?"

She nods.

"I passed her on the corner. How are you doing?"

"Not good." She tells how she woke in the morning with a terrible pain in her left upper leg that moved to her buttocks and lower back. At dialysis, when she looked at the clock and couldn't see any numbers, Roxanne the RN told her it might be a mini stroke. For a few hours, she lost all vision in her left eye. Her vision is back now, Charlene says, but her pain remains.

Beverly, the dialysis technician, asked, "Is there anything I can do for you, Char?"

"Yes, you can give me a kick right here." Charlene pointed to her upper leg.

"Oh, I could never do that."

"Well, you asked what you could do."

Instead, Bev brought a blanket and put it under the hurting leg to relieve the pressure on the hamstring. The pain went away, and Charlene thought she was better until she got up and tried to walk. Then, the pain came shooting back. Bev had to wheel her out to her vehicle.

"Joyce was so sweet and precious as she drove me home," Charlene says. "Almost as precious as you. But I don't love her like I do you."

Joyce helped her into the house and put the phone on the table for her so she could reach it if she needed to call someone.

Now, I let Nibaa out of her crate, put Charlene's first taco together, and split a pain pill in half to make it easier for her to swallow. Charlene moves into the living room and turns on her oxygen.

"I thought about asking you to stay overnight. But no, I'll be okay."

"Would you like me to stay overnight? I'll stay overnight."

"It would make me feel better." She pushes one tennis shoe off, then the other. Leans down, pulls up one of her pant legs, and starts, slowly, to push the long knee sock down her leg. "When you pray for me, tell God I'm at the end of my tolerance."

"Can I help you with that?" I kneel beside her and pull the socks slowly down her legs, one tug at a time, and then hold her moccasins in place while she slips her feet into them. I squat back and look up at her.

She is smiling, the love in her eyes like halos. "I don't think your parents could love you more than I do. I love you so much and I'm so proud of you. Out of all the people I've known my entire life—the people I've lived with, even—I've never known anyone as sweet as you."

"Thank you, Char." Warmth encircles my heart. She is proud of me. No words could mean more.

At work, my shift is hectic. Not only is my wing short-staffed, a few hours into the shift, a resident falls and has to be taken downstairs to the emergency room. The night clicks along with barely time for a thought of Charlene, but I do call Mom and ask her to pray.

I stop at Walmart after my shift to buy a contact case. Everything else I need I keep in an overnight bag at Charlene's house, at her suggestion. When I arrive at her house, it's bright with light and nestled into snow like a scene from a Christmas snow globe. Charlene sits at her table, fully dressed, playing solitaire.

"I fell asleep in my recliner and just woke up five minutes ago," she says.

I let whimpering Nibaa outside and sit down at the table with an apple and peanut butter. We talk while I scrape the last of the peanut butter from the jar and spread it on my apple. "I'll have to buy more."

I like the familiarity of saying these words, the sense of this being my house, my peanut butter. I probably ate more of it than Charlene did, after all. This house, which not long ago I thought smoke-filled and hostile, has become my second home.

Charlene moves into the living room to sit in her recliner. I dress in my red pajamas and Charlene's fuzzy teal bathrobe and wash my face with a scratchy, smoky-smelling washcloth from the stack in her bathroom. I go into the living room to braid my hair. I want her to see its long glossiness and admire it.

She sits rigid in her recliner. Her eyes carry that bright hard look of pain.

"I hurt so bad, Luci."

I kneel beside her. "Do you want to pray together?"

She nods. I remember my bare head—I always cover it when I pray—and wonder if I should get my bandana. But I don't want to spoil the moment. Charlene asked me about my covering once, and when I gave her the verses in Corinthians from which the teaching was taken, she was scornful. "You mean to tell me that God wants me to wear a covering?" she said, as though I just suggested that God was asking her to brush her teeth. I didn't press the subject.

Forgive me, God, I breathe, *for praying uncovered*. With my left hand, I hold Charlene's hand, small and cold, the fingers dry below the purple nails. My right hand rests on her upper arm.

"Dear God, you know Char is in so much pain. She can't take any more. Please take away her pain. Thank you for giving her to me and thank you that she is such a good friend. Thank you for bringing our lives together. Thank you that you love us so much, and please take away her pain, dear Lord. In Jesus's name, amen."

Charlene remains silent for a long moment until I wonder if she will pray. Then, she begins. I watch her the first bit as she prays with head bowed and eyes closed. Hair dark behind her, tiny face wrinkled and deep with the stillness of Indian, to me beloved. Her words spoken in a soft, childlike voice.

"Dear Lord, thank you for my dear friend Luci. You saved the best for last, and for that I thank you. I hurt so bad, but this is always my prayer, that not my will but yours be done. Please let this pain end and take me to heaven where I can see you. Then, in the twinkling of an eye, Luci will be there, and she'll be able to know me when I'm healthy. In Jesus's name, amen."

She lifts her head and looks at me intently. "And that is my eternal prayer. I feel sad that you've only known me when I'm a crotchety old lady." She smiles the wrinkly-eyed, twinkly-eyed Char smile. "I'm actually a lot of fun."

"You're not a crotchety old lady. Anyway, I know you for what you really are—young and joyful and fun and beautiful."

She smiles, pleased. "I wish we could have known each other when I wasn't so puny."

I imagine a younger Charlene, without pain. Maybe what I imagine is a Charlene who never was. One who laughs from her stomach, who lifts her head in thunderstorms, who tips her head back and gurgles life down her throat like water until she is flush and glowing with it. One who speaks clearly and commands respect. Charlene as she is, but without the past anger. I would like to know a Charlene like that.

But now I am thinking of something else.

"We would have never gotten to be friends if you were still young. Because we're so different. That's what brought us together. You needed help, and I needed someone to help."

She shrugs. Maybe.

"You're an interesting person, Char. I like interesting people."

She smiles without moving her lips, that pleased, inside-her-face smile with only her wrinkles turning up.

I hug her, gentle with her stiff, pain-filled body. "I love you so much and am so proud of you, too, Char. I'll go to bed now, but yell for me if you need anything. Even if it's a little thing."

She nods.

I sleep hard and wake at 5:00, worried about Charlene. I peek into the living room to see if she's sitting in her recliner. She isn't. She must still be in bed. I return to mine, but two minutes later, the kitchen light flips on. I get up again and go out.

"Did you sleep?" I ask.

"No."

"Did you call me in the night?" I realize guiltily that if she did, I slept right through it.

"No. But I'm surprised you didn't hear the yell I let out when I got into bed last night. The pain was so bad."

"No, I didn't hear it. I sleep like the dead."

We talk early morning talk at the table. We read our Bibles together, Charlene working through hers like clockwork, me reading more slowly. Afterward, she tells me how angry she feels with God.

"I think he must have given up on me because I'm not learning patience. I've given up alcohol, ninety percent of my swearing, and I do things in moderation. And I get a broken-down, old body when I'm seventy."

"I was reading from Job this morning," I say. "And this was one of the study notes. 'Suffering helps us love God for what he is, and not what he does for us.'"

"Maybe I'm fighting a battle against Satan."

"That's exactly right," I say. "That's exactly what Satan would tell you, that God has given up on you. He's a wolf. He attacks the ones that are down and weak."

"I've never felt such love as I have with your family. I've learned in life that people don't care about you. Nobody does. But every person in your family cares about me. Even your grandpa and grandma."

"That makes me happy, to know you feel that with us."

She moves to her recliner and sits with her oxygen tank, watching television, while I drive to the hardware store for tung oil to gloss her magazine rack. Charlene, being original, doesn't keep her magazine rack in the living room, filled with magazines, as one would expect. Instead, she keeps it in her bathroom, next to the washer and dryer, holding a single box of dryer sheets. She examined the magazine rack recently, ran her fingers over its dry, unpolished wood, and decided it needed a coat of tung oil.

When I get back with the oil, I spread newspaper on the floor next to her recliner and bring the magazine rack from the bathroom so I can work beside her.

"Now, where are you going to start?"

I think about it. "On the bottom."

"And where next?"

"I'll start on the bottom and work up to the top."

"And get the inside first," Charlene says. "That's how I do things. I think about how I'm going to do it before I start."

She speaks in a calm and gentle voice, and because she hasn't raised my defenses, I understand for the first time her preciseness. I've always before viewed it as nit-pickiness and a desire for control. But no. Charlene thinks about how she will do something, and then she does it. She doesn't, like me, start in the middle and figure it out as she goes along.

She watches, sharp-eyed and interested, as I begin the spreading of the tung.

"I guess I should have done this in the bathroom so you couldn't watch me," I say.

She looks away, not watching too much. After a few moments, she utters a short exclamation.

"Are you okay?"

"Yes. My eyes are slamming shut."

I look at her blankly.

"I'm about to fall asleep," she translates.

So she sleeps while I finish the project.

When I am done, I rise to leave, anxious to be home and about my business. "I'll see you tomorrow. Call if you need anything." I pick up my purse. "I love you!" I call from the doorway.

She leans forward from her recliner in the living room, leaning so she can see me at the kitchen door. Her face is encased in smiled gentleness, wrinkles massed on her cheeks. "I love you more!" she crows.

My free-spirited, open-hearted Char.

How I love that old woman.

The next morning, I call her the minute I wake up. "How are you doing?"

"Not good, Luci. I need you to come. I can't do anything. It took me half an hour to get dressed."

"Okay, I'll get ready and be right up."

I cancel my scheduled cleaning job and dress for the day. Before I can get out the door, she calls a second time.

"I called Mary, and she said I shouldn't wait for you—that I should call the ambulance right away and go into the emergency room."

"Okay. I'll come to the hospital, then."

"Would you stop and feed Nibaa first?"

"Sure."

At the hospital, I hesitate at the swinging ER doors, then push through to the desk and the lady behind it. "I've come to see Charlene Brand?"

"In the room to your right."

I step into the room. A curtain blocks my view, but Charlene lies just on the other side of it. She smiles when she sees me.

I touch her hand. "Sorry. My hands are cold."

She wraps her fingers around mine. "I don't care if they're cold. I need to hang on to something."

We sit holding hands while I watch Charlene in amazement. The last time I saw her in this hospital, she was a bear, a she-wolf crouched outside its den, wounded and snarling.

Charlene hates places like this, fears them. Mary was furious with her in her last emergency for absolutely refusing to ride in the ambulance. Now, in this extremity, she is Nathan Hale, Sydney Carton, Jesus—meeting her nemesis willingly. She called the ambulance, she came alone to this place she hates, and, in the face of intense pain, she is smiling and cracking jokes with the RN.

The nurse's short hair arches from her head like a rooster tail, and she seems delighted to have such an amenable patient. "You've got spunk. I love when we get people like you. I just give that playful attitude right back."

The doctor comes and taps around on Charlene's legs. Her face contorts from the pain and, beside her, I wince. He puts his stethoscope against her legs beneath the thin hospital gown, listening, but unable to find circulation in either one. The nurse listens next. "I hear a little," she says.

"I believe you." He looks at Charlene straight. "I'm making arrangements to send you to the hospital in Eau Claire. You could lose one or both of your legs."

While he leaves to make his phone calls, Joyce, Charlene's dialysis driver and good friend, arrives. She sits beside Charlene's bed on a little stool, pleasant, making conversation, making normal.

"Isn't she just precious?" Charlene asks when Joyce steps out of the room for a phone call.

I nod.

"But I don't love her like I do you."

Joyce is precious. She jokes with Charlene. She gives me directions to the hospital. She smiles. She is normal. She leaves right before the EMTs come.

I tell Charlene I'll follow the ambulance in my car.

"Would you drop my things off and bring my Bible?"

"Sure. I can do that, Char."

I drive to her place, pick up her Bible and my overnight bag, fill the car with gas, and stop at McDonald's for a sandwich. Snow is falling now and the roads have grown slushy, but visibility is good. I drive almost my normal speed, and so does everyone else. We Wisconsinites are not stopped by simple white stuff.

An hour later, I find a spot in the parking garage outside the hospital and walk the long labyrinth of hallways to the ER—passing paintings, carpets, a coffee shop, and smiling blonde nurses. I am glad for the familiarity and friendliness of this place, glad Charlene and I can be here, if we have to be in a hospital, and not in some stark, strange place.

At the ER, a nurse gives me Charlene's room number and tells me not to go inside until the surgeon is through talking to her. I sit on a flowered chair in the waiting room, feeling jittery. Charlene will wonder where I am.

People stream in and out of her door. I hear one RN tell another that he's been unable to draw her blood. Then his pager sounds. "Code Blue, Code Blue. Room 201." The two nurses run off down the hallway, the blood-drawing RN pushing his equipment in front of him.

Finally, the surgeon steps out of Charlene's room. He is smiling, humor in his eyes. I wonder what she's been saying to him.

I go in, my body reaching.

Charlene's black hair sprawls behind her on the bed. Her eyes greet me with their warmth, every wrinkle glad. "There's that little Luci."

"How are you doing, Char?"

"Well, they finally got me something for the pain, so I'm much better than I was."

The surgeon had said she'd "spit out a blood clot," but instead of traveling to her brain, it traveled down her left leg. So now he'll make an incision in her groin where the main artery begins and send a miniscule probe down to try to draw it out. If that doesn't work, he'll try again lower, below the knee. After that, he'll look for deterioration in the muscle. The longer blood hasn't circulated to her leg, the greater the chance it's beyond saving.

"If it's too far gone, then *shwwwp*." She makes a slashing motion across the leg.

Guilt lies heavy on my heart. "I'm sorry I didn't bring you in yesterday."

"Oh, honey, it wasn't your fault. I won't go to the doctor unless I have to. If I get sick, I know I should go to the doctor, but I keep waiting, hoping it will get better. Then it gets worse, and I end up at the doctor's anyway. Don't blame yourself."

"Well, I'm not going to worry about it." It's too late now, anyway.

"Good. And if it's the Creator's will that I lose my leg, I would be okay with that."

I cannot comprehend such a possibility. Charlene will be fine, as she always is, because she needs to be. In pain, yes, but whole Char, my Char. She's been through hell, this woman, and always, she is fine.

A red-haired man comes in and introduces himself as the anesthesiologist. He asks Charlene to lift her chin and open her mouth wide so he can see her airway. "We won't use general anesthesia unless there are complications, but I need to take a look just in case."

Charlene complies.

"Looks real good," he says.

"Room for you to get your finger in there," she says.

He smiles. "I do use three fingers as my measuring tool, so yeah."

"I asked that Dr. Erickson if he minded second billing," Charlene says. "He looked at me like, 'What's this crazy old woman talking about?' 'Because you'll do everything you can do, but it's in the Creator's hands whether I live or die,' I told him. 'I don't mind second billing,' he said."

The man listens, intent. "You come first with Dr. Erickson. And with me too."

"Dr. Erickson was snippy with me at first," Charlene tells me, when the anesthesiologist has gone. "Very curt. He had to show me he was professional, but I know he is only an educated guesser. He chastised me about waiting two days before I came in. And he yelled at me about my five cigarettes a day. I get so tired of that. I told him I have so much wrong with me, if I came in every time I felt a little something, I would be coming in all the time. And I told him when my sister bought me a pack of cigarettes, she bought me one of those fake cigarettes, so I can quit smoking. I thought I'd better show him I'm his friend if he'll be doing the surgery."

I remember how the surgeon was smiling when he stepped out of the room. She must have been successful with her overtures of friendship.

Mom calls and I let her talk to Charlene. "God bless you and I love you," Charlene says before she hangs up.

An RN named Lindsay comes in with a transport lady to take Charlene to surgery. The transport lady wears a silly snowman stocking cap.

"I like your hat!" Charlene says.

The lady laughs. "It fits today."

"Do you have any personal items you want along?" Lindsay asks. "You'll be in a different unit afterward."

Charlene looks at me. "Luci has them."

"No, I don't. I dropped your things off at your place, like you told me to."

"Well, then I'll just have to run home naked!"

I laugh, my full, happy laugh.

She smiles, pleased.

Lindsay and the transport lady smile too. They are probably not used to encountering such casual relaxation on the brink of a major emergency.

It's all Charlene. I follow her lead, amazed. Every other time I've been in a hospital with her she's been a tight snarling cat ball of fear and defensiveness. Today, she is not. She is strong, humorous, relaxed.

I walk beside the bed with her small cold hand in mine as the transport lady wheels it down the smooth hallways, our heels clicking on tile floors. We smile at the people we pass, a sort of misty-close threesome encircled in a moment of our own, like a TV commercial. The transport lady tells me to ask for a pager at the nurses' station, so I can get updates on the surgery.

"Make sure you call Mary and let her know what's going on," Charlene says.

I nod.

Outside the door marked OR, I give her a hug and a kiss.

"I'll see you later, Char." I say this to make it true, and to let her know I believe it to be true. "I love you and I'll be praying for you."

She smiles, satisfied. "I love you too. And I'm glad I got to talk to your mom."

After her bed disappears through the double doors, I walk on down the hallway and find the desk and the surgical waiting area. I get my pager and call Mary with an update. I wait an hour before the pager beeps, and then I go to the desk and talk on the provided telephone to Charlene's nurse. The surgery is going fine, the nurse says, but taking longer than expected. They want to do some angiograms, which means they'll insert dye into Charlene's artery and follow it to see if they can find the blood clot that way.

After I hang up the phone, the receptionist leans forward and catches my eye. "I wanted to compliment you," she said. "I'm sure this must be a difficult time for you, and you are so calm."

But I have not pulled the calmness from any deep well of strength I possess. I lean on Charlene, the sick woman, calm because she is calm. If she were tense, I also would be. I remember the rivers of tears I cried during our last hospital visit. This time, contrary to her circumstances, she seems stronger and happier than I've ever seen her. Her strength amazes me, and it is this strength I lean into.

I blame myself for not bringing her in sooner, but I know Charlene doesn't blame me. "It is up to the Creator," she said. And because she trusts the Creator, I also do.

I wait hours that way, trusting, reading the book I picked up at Charlene's house, a Zane Gray western. She loves his stories, but I never paid attention to him before. Now I read, letting the words slip easily into my mind, the book a small connection with my friend. The hours are caught in some web of timelessness—a netherworld of bright lights, of sipping cappuccino, of watching the others leave the surgical waiting room area one by one, of believing I will be next. My pager will beep anytime, I know. I will see Charlene and she will be fine. Finally, it is dark outside, and I am the only one left.

Mary and her husband Ron come at last. It feels good not to be alone anymore, good to have capable Mary talking, worrying about Charlene, asking what we're going to do if she loses her leg.

The doctor comes out at midnight to tell us the details of the long surgery. He tried to clean the blockage from her veins, but there was no blockage, only occlusion—calcium build-up caused by years of smoking.

"Char smoked since she was sixteen," Mary says. "And most of those years she smoked the unfiltered kind."

I always knew I hated those cigarettes. Now I know why.

"I have to make a decision," Dr. Erickson says, "as to whether or not she loses her legs. They can't get a blood pressure, and they want to put in a catheter to her bone so they can find it. If they do, she will surely lose her legs. If they don't, she will probably die."

So they're talking two legs now, not just one. I cannot imagine dogged little Char—my Char!—without legs and without the small amount of independence she possesses. She won't be able to sit on the garden cart to weed her flower bed, walk into the grocery store, or even walk herself along the cupboards from the recliner to the bathroom. I won't be able to take care of her, and she'll have to go to the nursing home, like so many other helpless elderly people I've seen.

But Charlene isn't like other people. She needs freedom. Without legs, the life that propels her body and shines from her eyes, the will that makes her get out of bed in the mornings when she's hurting, her joy in sunshine and flowers and thunderstorms and air and in doing things ... without legs, her life will be gone.

For the second time in my life, I pray she will die.

After Dr. Erickson leaves, Mary asks if she can talk to my mom on the phone. She's never met my mom before. "I don't know what to do," she says.

I dial my home number, and Mom answers. "Mary wants to talk to you."

Mary tells Mom she doesn't know how to decide, if the doctor asks her, about Charlene's legs.

"Maybe God will make it clear so we don't have to decide," Mom says.

A man with glasses and a still, soft face comes out and sits on the edge of a chair. He introduces himself as the chaplain and makes pleasant conversation. "What was Char's life like before her surgery?" he asks. "Did she have a good quality of life? Did she experience a lot of pain?"

He is preparing us, I think.

Mary talks, telling her memories, and my words tumble into hers. Sharing the memories is healing, even with this complete stranger. As a private person, I wouldn't have guessed how good it can feel to talk.

"How is she doing?" Mary asks. "Do you know?"

The chaplain hesitates. "I can't say."

Dr. Erickson comes toward us down the hallway and stands in front of us. "She is gone. We couldn't get a blood pressure on her. She passed away in the OR. I'm so sorry."

But she is still whole. And I am thankful, so thankful. Charlene won't have to wake up to a life with no legs.

Dr. Erickson's eyes are weary—his whole body weary, his face defeated.

"We know you did what you could," Ron says. "Thank you."

The doctor stays a few minutes for questions, and then he is gone down the long hallway.

And then Mary is hugging me and crying, saying, "You'll help me now, won't you, Luci?"

"Yes," I say, and mean it, thinking all the love and loyalty I gave Charlene I'll give to Mary, for Charlene's sake. Char loved her. But I am awkward, bent at a funny angle over a chair while Mary hugs me. I dare not move for fear of ruining the moment. My empty Styrofoam coffee cup, perched on the arm of the chair, falls to the floor. I am conscious of it and conscious of how I must look, bent at this odd angle, with Mary crying, and my own face as clear and unwashed as blue summer sky. How do people cry so easily?

We separate, and I bend down to pick up the coffee cup.

I am glad Charlene is gone. She was in so much pain, and now she's free. And now maybe I can have a little freedom too.

I wanna live again, I think, as I've thought so often in the past year when I wondered if I would ever have space to breathe, to be selfish, to write, to travel, to go on the mission field.

I go around the corner to call my mom, and that is when I cry. Out of eyesight, by myself with the coffee machine, the crying comes—the deep sobs, the contorted face, the body writhing against the wall.

"Char is dead," I tell Mom, managing that. "But she was ready to go. She was glad she got to talk to you. She said it was in the hands of the Creator."

I hang up the phone and tuck away the tears. I walk back out to the others and even smile. I can do this, and it doesn't bother me, because I am separate from my emotions, dwelling in that same netherworld I've inhabited all day, of bright lights and unreality.

We talk to the chaplain a long time, sharing memories and hearing his soothing affirmations. "When can we see Char?" Mary finally asks. He goes to find out and comes back to lead us through smooth silent hallways, past quiet nighttime nurses. We step into a room, and her body is there, lying on a bed.

She is gone.

I loved that body so much. I look at it, disbelieving it is only empty body and Charlene is not there. But the face is expressionless. The spirit has flown. I will not see Charlene again. Not in the morning, not in the evening after. The truth is hard to believe. Hard ... hard ... hard to believe. As outside my comprehension as an absence of God.

Mary and Ron stand on one side of the bed, I on the other. I hold Charlene's hand, feel how the fingers curl naturally around mine. You would hardly know she is dead, by her hand. It's only a little cold ... and Charlene is always cold.

Tubes still connect to her arms. Her mouth is open and twisted to one side, stuffed with the thing—whatever it's called—they put in during anesthesia to prop it open. I remember the anesthesiologist, with his three fingers, his red hair, and glasses.

Her hands and arms are heavily bruised from the surgery team's efforts to take her blood pressure.

None of us want to look at her legs.

I am glad she will not wake up to the bruises and cuts. She's always endured pain, but now it is gone. She doesn't have to come back to that, and I am happy. Happy, happy, happy. So happy. The tears mean nothing. I am happy.

Her hair remains black in death as it was in life, mussed and wild. I touch her forehead and her hair. I want to kiss her. Kiss her on her face, her forehead, her ear, her lips, run my fingers down her soft cheek. But I don't. Because she's dead. And Mary and Ron are there. And there is something gross about kissing a dead body.

I only hold her hand. I let the fingers curl and uncurl around my fingers, stroke the hand, touch the hair and the side of the face. I am glad the fingers still curl. They fit naturally into mine, as though they have never left.

Mary and Ron talk to her, tell her goodbye. Mary walks out first, then Ron, and then me. I do not tell her goodbye. It would be pointless because Charlene is dead. I do not want her spirit to be hanging around vile earth, listening for empty words. I want her to be free and forgetful, swinging in heaven with Jesus. And so I will not talk to her.

I do not talk to her until months later, sitting in her empty house, soon to be sold, tears running down my cheeks. Then I tell her every single thing I am thinking. I tell her the things I would never have told her when she was alive, as though I am talking to God. I don't know if she hears me. I don't really want her to hear. The words are free-form and embarrassing. But I ask God to relay the message. "Tell her I love her."

It is only after I talk to her out loud, and tell her goodbye, that I am able to let her go. I open my heart and watch her spirit flutter out the window, into space.

Mary tells me, "Our brother John sexually molested her when she was a girl." We sit side by side on an old van seat in Mary's basement, Charlene's things piled in boxes beside us. "She didn't tell you? I thought she would have."

I am angry. Angry. Angry. For the first time, what I sensed falls into place. Charlene's anger at John, how she said he ruined her life, and her oblique statement, "The things people did to me that were wrong, I could have stopped them at any time. So I was just as wrong."

Some part deep inside me knew it, I think—some nodule of my heart and spirit—but my brain, slower and stupider than the rest of my senses, never put it into words.

I think of her first date at the skating park, and how she said it wasn't exciting. Of course it wasn't. She already knew too much. For Charlene, there was no attraction in the opposite sex, no mystery left.

I remember how I sat across from her and talked with my large ruby red lips—callous lips—and told her I thought of sex as sacred, like a rose opening, and that I would only want to give myself to a very special person whom I loved very much.

"I know you would," she said, warmly. Admiring, as though she thought it was I who was sacred.

She never had the chance to wait.

For her, sex became a commodity, traded between partners for pleasure, for companionship ... for love. But who had loved her, really, while doing it with her? By the time she was seventy, they had gone.

I wonder now about another obsession of hers: murder.

"I think murdering someone must be the worst sin," she said to me once.

"I think the worst sin is when someone molests a child," I said.

She looked thoughtful for a few moments before saying, "Yes, I suppose taking a child's innocence is about on a par with taking a life."

But she never laid the question down. She asked it to me more than once, brought it to Bible study and asked it there. A simple question, intently asked. "Could God forgive a murderer?"

In earlier, unenlightened days, I thought she was asking for theoretical reasons, or perhaps because a great-uncle murdered someone and swept the deed into his pants pocket, with only Charlene as his secret-carrier. But now I know Charlene, and I've never known her to concern herself with others' responsibilities. She asked for herself.

I don't know why, but I can guess. And if I am right, it would be like her to put the deed into one awful word, blunt and unblushing. Murder. As though she herself went into her body with a knife and twisted it around in her womb and stood up triumphant with a limp tadpole of a fetus impaled on the point of her knife.

I can't understand Jake.

I hadn't realized the four years he is younger than me would make such a difference, that I would feel so old and that he would seem so young.

He focuses on details, wants to discuss liberal versus conservative and whether Christians should listen to contemporary music. Music! When children are being abused.

I think of Charlene, of how she loved me. In comparison, Jake seems cold, an alien beaming in to check me out and see if I pass muster or if my planet must be destroyed. If only he would love me! As Char did.

I know it's my fault, know I am not the innocent young girl he expected from when he knew me before. Thinking of all I experienced with Charlene—the emotions, the passion, the eye-opening knowledge—I feel dirty and unclean.

I can be that innocent girl again, for his sake. I know I can because I love him. I chose him so long ago. In the darkness of his truck one night, the engine idling where he came to drop me off, Jake tells me our relationship isn't working for him. "We're just going down two different paths," he says.

I think his face looks distant, and I feel cold and disbelieving, as though this is someone else's life, as though it is a book. Maybe I will write about it.

Sitting there beside him in the truck, I feel as I have come to feel so often since knowing Charlene—large and wild and un-Mennonite. Two different paths, he said. I wonder if he thinks I am going to hell. Or perhaps only one of its suburbs. I climb slowly out of the truck.

"Blessings to your life," he says.

Leaning up against a tree later, my body heaving, I tell God I am sorry. "I'm sorry for all the times I hurt Char. I just didn't know how it felt."

A week later, I attend a writers' conference, open my mind to the old dreams of writing, and realize I am free. I fill my mouth with the freedom and taste it against the rough bumps of my tongue. Charlene bound me, Jake stifled me, but now, for the first time in over two years, I am free. The summer air smells of honeysuckle and grass seed and delight. I am running barefoot in a hayfield, the wind in my face, the prickly grass stalks stinging my feet.

This is life. I am young still. I have a book to write.

Charlene always told me no one would come to her funeral, but at her memorial service, nieces and nephews she'd helped through the years packed the funeral home. Whatever her faults, they knew she loved them.

Mary asked my dad to preach, and he did—a simple message of hope and salvation. My family stood to sing the song they sang with her once in her little house: "I shall know him, I shall know him, by the prints of the nails in his hands." Her nephews played the drums. And when it was time to share our memories, I got up and told them what she always said she'd be doing right now—taking care of the baby elephants.

Soon after Charlene died, Sondra had a dream where she saw her running across a green field, her legs strong and free. I like to think of her like that.

She asked me for a turtle heart, and I like to think she got what she wanted, that when she walked on to the other side, her old heart was reborn, new blood pumped through her veins, that she threw back her head and laughed for joy, the old anger forgotten. "See," she will say, when I see her again. "This is what it means to be born again."

Only she won't. We won't be thinking of stuff like that.

The Ojibwe say the earth is built on the back of a turtle, and if they say this, maybe it is because they know a turtle's heart, like the earth, beats almost forever. But there is one earthly thing which lasts longer, and that is a soul.

Char's spirit lives on. Her heart still beats in the memories of us who loved her, in the lessons she taught us, in the stories we tell.

I still am not sure how to view our relationship. Like Charlene said, people always try to put a label on things. This one didn't fit a label.

She was my mentor, my equal, my grandma, my sister, my loudest detractor, my strongest supporter. In the most basic sense of our friendship, down below the thoughts and words, we came together because we needed each other. Charlene was my teacher. Charlene was my child.

I learned from her it is wrong to couch God in religious phrases or holster him in churches when he is near enough to touch, found in the primal things of life that even a child can understand. I need not go looking for him. He is here, basic to my needs and my senses. I can learn of his ways from the people near me. I can see him in everyday life, in the wind and the trees and the smiles of children and the quiet sure voice that tells me to forgive. He is present in small ways in small things as much as and more than he is present in large ways in large things. Because it is his presence that keeps those small things—each revolution of every atom, each beat of every heart, the relentless tender life which bursts from earth—in motion. Miracles are nothing.

With her, I also learned there are some places in another human soul we can never touch or understand. Friendship is the crossing over, the bridge, the stepping across the gap of what is known and what is unknown, what is understood and what is bewildering.

Friendship takes two. I cannot build this bridge alone. I thought I was building a bridge to Char but turns out she was building a bridge to me.

We call that love, and it is the most mysterious, most powerful force in the world. We also call it God.

ABOUT THE AUTHOR

LUCINDA J KINSINGER has always viewed herself as a shy little Mennonite girl, but refuses to let that stop her from pursuing what she loves—whether that's writing with honesty and vulnerability or traveling to a remote village in China. She is the author of *Anything But Simple: My Life as a Mennonite* and *The Arrowhead*. Lucinda married Ivan in November 2019 and currently makes her home in the rolling hills of Garrett County, Maryland. She writes a column for *Anabaptist World Review* and blogs at lucindajkinsinger. com.

REFERENCES

In *Turtle Heart*, many partial Bible verses are quoted. In the following reference list, these verses have been written in full along with the accompanying page number. Other irregularities are noted in parentheses.

Part One—The Birth

23 Where their worm dieth not, and the fire is not quenched." (Mark 9:44)("The" replaces "their" in text.)

26 That if thou shalt confess with thy mouth the Lord Jesus, and shalt believe in thine heart that God hath raised him from the dead, thou shalt be saved. (Romans 10:9)

26 If we confess our sins, he is faithful and just to forgive us our sins, and to cleanse us from all unrighteousness. (1 John 1:9)

42 And Mary said, My soul doth magnify the Lord, And my spirit hath rejoiced in God my Saviour. (Luke 1:46–47)

51 The heart is deceitful above all things and desperately wicked: who can know it? (Jeremiah 17:9)

51 If a man say, I love God, and hateth his brother, he is a liar: for he that loveth not his brother whom he hath seen, how can he love God whom he hath not seen? And this commandment have we from him, That he who loveth God love his brother also. (1 John 4:20–21) (In the text, this is misquoted as "He who loves God loves his brother also.")

80 Teaching them to observe all things whatsoever I have commanded you: and, lo, I am with you alway, even unto the end of the world. Amen. (Matthew 28:20) ("Always" replaces "alway" in text.)

80 In my Father's house are many mansions: if it were not so, I would have told you. I go to prepare a place for you. And if I go and prepare a place for you, I will come again, and receive you unto myself; that where I am, there ye may be also. (John 14:2–3)

80 And God shall wipe away all tears from their eyes; and there shall be no more death, neither sorrow, nor crying, neither shall there be any more pain: for the former things are passed away. (Revelation 21:4)

86 Set me as a seal upon thine heart, as a seal upon thine arm: for love is strong as death; jealousy is cruel as the grave: the coals thereof are coals of fire, which hath a most vehement flame. Many waters cannot quench love, neither can the floods drown it: if a man would give all the substance of his house for love, it would utterly be contemned. (Song of Solomon 8:6–7)

99 And the Lord God said, It is not good that the man should be alone; I will make him an help meet for him. (Genesis 2:18) (Text replaces "an" with "a.")

134 For this cause God gave them up unto vile affections: for even their women did change the natural use into that which is against nature: And likewise also the men, leaving the natural use of the woman, burned in their lust one toward another; men with men working that which is unseemly, and receiving in themselves that recompence of their error which was meet. (Romans 1:26–27)

134 Thou shalt not lie with mankind, as with womankind: it is abomination. (Leviticus 18:22)

134 If a man also lie with mankind, as he lieth with a woman, both of them have committed an abomination: they shall surely be put to death; their blood shall be upon them. (Leviticus 20:13)

Part Three—Things Desired

175 Thou shalt have no other gods before me ... Thou shalt not bow down thyself to them, nor serve them: for I the LORD thy God am a jealous God. (Exodus 20:3, 5a) (These verses have been paraphrased in the text, and "LORD thy God" is replaced by the original Hebrew names.)

177 Ye shall know them by their fruits. (Matthew 7:16a)

179 Remember the Sabbath day to keep it holy. (Exodus 20:8)

180 Saying, Father, if thou be willing, remove this cup from me: nevertheless not my will, but thine, be done. (Luke 22:42)

185 Charity suffereth long, and is kind; charity envieth not ... is not easily provoked, thinketh no evil; Rejoiceth not in iniquity, but rejoiceth in the truth; Beareth all things, believeth all things, hopeth all things, endureth all things ... Charity never faileth. (1 Corinthians 13:4–8) (Excerpts. "Fails" replaces "faileth" in the text.)

190 Max Ehrman, "Desiderata," 1927.

228 For as the heavens are higher than the earth, so are my ways higher than your ways, and my thoughts than your thoughts. (Isaiah 55:9)

228 Yea, though I walk through the valley of the shadow of death, I will fear no evil: for thou art with me; thy rod and thy staff they comfort me. (Psalm 23:4)

229 *My Savior First of All,* Fanny Crosby, 1894.

Part Four—New Birth

262 For by grace are ye saved through faith; and that not of yourselves, it is the gift of God: Not of works, lest any man should boast. For we are his workmanship, created in Christ Jesus unto good works, which God hath before ordained that we should walk in them. (Ephesians 2:8–10)

263 But we are all as an unclean thing, and all our righteousnesses are as filthy rags; and we all do fade as a

leaf; and our iniquities, like the wind, have taken us away. (Isaiah 64:6) ("Righteousness" replaces "righteousnesses" in the text.)

Manufactured by Amazon.ca
Bolton, ON

20675589R00175